Why are there

882½

answers
in this book?

1

Because the Titanic *was 882 ½ feet long!*

First published in Great Britain in 1999 by Little, Brown and Company (UK)

Produced by
Madison Press Books
40 Madison Avenue
Toronto
Ontario
Canada M5R 2S1

0 316 85158 2

A CIP catalogue record for this book
is available from the British Library.

Little, Brown and Company (UK)
Brettenham House
Lancaster Place
London WC2E 7EN

Printed and bound by G. Canale & C., Torino, Italy

882½ AMAZING ANSWERS to your QUESTIONS about the TITANIC

By **HUGH BREWSTER** and **LAURIE COULTER**

Text research by **GREG CURTIS** *Historical consultation by* **DON LYNCH**

Paintings by **KEN MARSCHALL**

A LITTLE, BROWN / MADISON PRESS BOOK

How long did it take the *Titanic* to sink?

At approximately 11:40 P.M. on April 14, 1912, the *Titanic* struck an iceberg. At 2:20 A.M. on April 15, roughly two hours and forty minutes later, the *Titanic* plunged to the bottom of the ocean. But what happened in those 160 minutes over 86 years ago has fascinated the world ever since.

BIRTH *of a* DREAM

Why was the *Titanic* so big?

3 At the beginning of this century, the only way to cross the ocean was by ship. Two British shipping companies, Cunard and White Star, competed fiercely for passengers. In 1907 Cunard completed the *Lusitania* and the *Mauretania*—luxurious ships that could cross the ocean in a record five days. What could the White Star Line do to top that? They decided to build three ships that would be the largest the world had ever seen. One of these would be the *Titanic*.

WHITE STAR LINE

ROYAL AND UNITED STATES
MAIL STEAMERS
LIVERPOOL · NEW YORK
LIVERPOOL · BOSTON
NEW YORK · MEDITERRANEAN
BOSTON · MEDITERRANEAN

Whose idea was it to build the *Titanic*?

4 The idea for the *Titanic* was born during a dinner party in the summer of 1907. It was held at the London mansion of Lord Pirrie, the chairman of Harland & Wolff shipbuilders, and attended by J. Bruce Ismay, the director of the White Star Line. Cunard's fast new liner, *Lusitania*, was the talk of the shipping world. After dinner, Pirrie and Ismay hatched a plan to build three huge ships, each one bigger and more luxurious than the *Lusitania*. The first ship would be called *Olympic*, the second, *Titanic*, and the third, *Gigantic*.

Who owned the *Titanic*?

5 Although the White Star Line was a British company, it was owned by wealthy American financier J.P. Morgan's trust, International Mercantile Marine (IMM). It was his money that bankrolled Pirrie and Ismay's dream of building three enormous new ships.

Just how big was the *Titanic*?

6 The *Titanic* was as long as four city blocks (882 ½ feet / 269 m) and as wide as a four-lane highway (92 ½ feet / 28 m). Its nine decks made it as tall as an eleven-story building. If stood on its end, the liner would have rivaled the tallest buildings of its day.

J. Bruce Ismay

Lord Pirrie

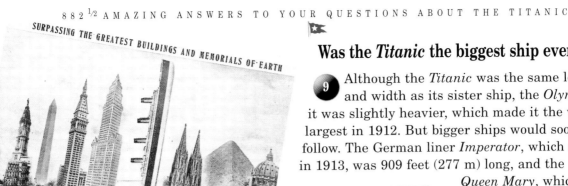

Was the *Titanic* the biggest ship ever built?

9 Although the *Titanic* was the same length and width as its sister ship, the *Olympic*, it was slightly heavier, which made it the world's largest in 1912. But bigger ships would soon follow. The German liner *Imperator*, which sailed in 1913, was 909 feet (277 m) long, and the *Queen Mary*, which made its first voyage in 1936, was over 1,000 feet (300 m) long. Several of today's giant cruise ships are even larger. For example, the *Grand Princess*, with 18 decks, is twice the size of the *Titanic*.

A 1912 postcard (above left) compares the Titanic *to the tallest buildings of its day, and a sign (above) boasts about its size.*

How much did it weigh?

7 It weighed over 53,000 tons (53,800 t).

How fast was the *Titanic* designed to go?

8 Its top speed was 24 knots, which is about the same as 28 miles per hour (45 kph) on land, but it never reached that speed on its maiden voyage.

Why did they name it the *Titanic*?

10 The Titans in Greek mythology were a legendary race of giants, so the word "titanic" means something huge. It was also the custom for White Star ships to have names ending in "-ic" (e.g., *Baltic*, *Majestic*) in contrast to Cunard's liners with their "-ia" names (e.g., *Mauretania, Lusitania*.)

Is it true that someone predicted the *Titanic* disaster?

11 The ship was a fabulous passenger liner, larger than any that had ever been built, and it was called unsinkable. Sailing across the North Atlantic in the month of April, with many rich and famous passengers aboard, it struck an iceberg and sank. Hundreds of passengers lost their lives because there were not enough lifeboats. The name of this ship? It was called the *Titan*. But it only existed in a novel called *Futility* by Morgan Robertson, published in 1898. Fourteen years later, the *Titanic* disaster would make this story come true.

BUILDING *the* GIANT

The Titanic *and its sister ship* Olympic *(right) were built side by side.*

Where did they build the *Titanic*?

12 The *Titanic* was built at Harland & Wolff shipyards in Belfast, Ireland. It was one of the largest shipyards in the world, but none of its slips (the sites where ships are constructed) were big enough to hold the new liners. Three of the old slips were combined into two giant new ones. Then a huge new gantry (a large metal framework) was built over the two slipways to aid construction. At 220 feet (67 m) high, it was the largest gantry in the world.

When did they start building the *Titanic*?

13 Work began on the *Titanic* on March 31, 1909.

The *Olympic* and *Titanic* were built side by side, but construction on the *Olympic* began three and a half months ahead of its sister ship.

Who built the *Titanic*?

14 Irish shipyard workers in Belfast. Over 15,000 people worked at Harland & Wolff. They began work at 7:50 A.M. and finished at 5:30 P.M., five days a week, plus a half day on Saturdays. They had a ten-minute mid-morning break and a half hour for lunch. They were given two days off at Christmas, two days at Easter, and a week of holidays in July—all without pay.

How much did the shipyard workers earn?

15 The average worker earned about £2 ($10) a week. The average wage at the time was £1 to £2 a week.

Harland & Wolff shipyards in Belfast, Ireland

What was the *Titanic* made of?

16 The *Titanic*'s hull was made of overlapping steel plates, 1 inch (3 cm) thick, fastened by over 3 million rivets.

How did they put in the rivets?

17 The iron rivets were 1 inch (3 cm) thick and 3 inches (8 cm) long. A worker nicknamed the "heater boy" would heat a rivet until it was red-hot. He would then throw it to the "catch boy," who caught it in a wooden bowl and placed it in a hole with a pair of tongs. While the "holder up" held a mallet over the rivet head on the outside of the hull, the "basher" on the inside of the hull would bash the rivet end into place.

How much did it cost to build the *Titanic*?

18 The approximate total construction cost for building the *Titanic* was $7.5 million, about $123 million in today's money.

Who designed the *Titanic*?

19 Thomas Andrews was head of Harland & Wolff's design department and oversaw the creation of the ship's plans. But company chairman Lord Pirrie controlled the *Titanic*'s overall design, while general manager Alexander Carlisle took charge of the details. At each stage, plans were sent to White Star director J. Bruce Ismay for his suggestions and approval.

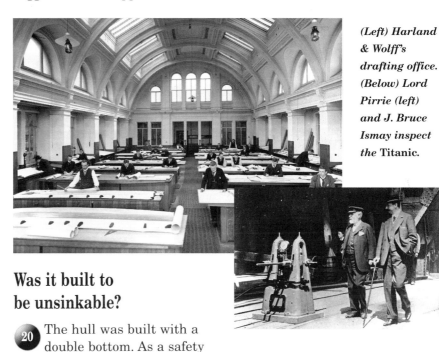

(Left) Harland & Wolff's drafting office. (Below) Lord Pirrie (left) and J. Bruce Ismay inspect the Titanic.

Was it built to be unsinkable?

20 The hull was built with a double bottom. As a safety feature, it was divided into 16 watertight compartments. The ship could stay afloat with any two of the middle compartments, or four of the first compartments, flooded. Since it was thought that even the worst collision would damage no more than two compartments, the *Titanic* was considered practically unsinkable.

Was someone sealed inside the hull by accident?

21 No. This is one of the many myths about the *Titanic*. Another is that a shipyard worker painted "We defy God to sink her" on her stern.

Shipyard workers pose in front of the **Olympic's** *hull.*

THE LARGEST OBJECT *ever* MOVED

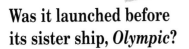

Launch
OF
White Star Royal Mail Triple-Screw Steamer
"TITANIC"
At BELFAST,
Wednesday, 31st May, 1911, at 12-15 p.m.
Admit Bearer.

When was the *Titanic* launched?

22 May 31, 1911.

Was it launched before its sister ship, *Olympic*?

23 No. The *Olympic* was launched on October 20, 1910.

With a ticket (above) you could watch the launch from inside the gantry.

Was it ready to sail on May 31?

24 No. The *Titanic* was just an empty hull at this stage.

How many people watched the launch?

25 More than 100,000 people crowded into the Harland & Wolff shipyard and stood along the banks of the River Lagan to watch the giant ship being moved into the water. Lord and Lady Pirrie, J.P. Morgan, J. Bruce Ismay, and their guests watched from a special grandstand.

How much did the hull weigh?

26 Twenty-six thousand tons (23,600 t).

Did this include the anchors?

27 Yes, the three largest anchors, which together weighed 31 tons/28 t (the weight of 20 cars), were installed before launching.

Why three anchors?

28 One for each side of the ship's bow and one center anchor that was stowed on the bow deck.

How much did each one weigh?

29 The center anchor weighed 15 ½ tons (14 t). It took a team of 20 horses to pull it into the shipyard.

30 The two side anchors weighed 7 ¾ tons (7 t) each.

Is it true someone was trapped under the hull?

31 Shortly before the *Titanic* was launched, the foremen blew whistles and the cry of "Stand clear!" was heard. The remaining workers rushed out from under the hull and the foremen counted their men. But James Dobbins was missing. A large wooden post had collapsed, pinning his leg beneath it. His fellow workers quickly found him and dragged him out. He died the next day, the second workman to die during the building of the *Titanic*.

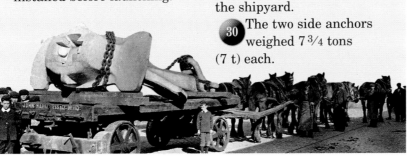

The red launch flag flutters on the stern as the new ship enters the river.

How did the shipyard workers move such a huge ship into the water?

32 The *Titanic* and the *Olympic* were built on 772-foot-long (235-m-long) wooden platforms (called "ways") that sloped gently down to the water. When the *Titanic* was ready to be launched, the workers greased the ways to make make them very slippery. The big posts holding the ship up were then knocked away, leaving the *Titanic* held in place with mechanical triggers. At a signal, the triggers would be released by the opening of a valve and the ship would slide down the ways into the river.

How much grease did it take?

33 Twenty-two tons (20 t) of tallow, soap, and train oil.

Was the *Titanic* really the largest object ever moved?

34 When the *Olympic* and the *Titanic* were launched, it was claimed that they were the largest man-made objects ever moved.

Did anyone smash a bottle of champagne on the *Titanic*'s bow?

35 No. Sometimes when a ship is launched an important person says, "I name this ship...", and a bottle of wine is broken on the bow. The White Star Line and Harland & Wolff did not have naming ceremonies at the launches of their ships.

Did they have fireworks instead?

36 Yes and no. When everything was ready, bright red rockets were exploded high into the air. But they had a practical purpose—to warn ships in the river to stay away from the launch area.

Then what happened?

37 Lord Pirrie gave the launch signals, a worker pulled the handle of the releasing valve, and the huge hull slipped down the ways into the water.

What stopped the ship from floating away?

39 Mammoth cables and the heavy anchors brought the *Titanic* to a standstill.

What happened after the launch?

40 Tugboats towed the *Titanic* to her berth in the outfitting basin.

41 Important guests and members of the press were treated to a roast beef dinner at Belfast's Grand Central Hotel.

42 The shipyard workers went back to work.

How long did this take?

38 Sixty-two seconds.

11

FITTING OUT

A final coat of paint is applied to the nearly completed ship in February 1912.

What does "fitting out" a ship mean?

43 Everything that is needed to make a ship ready for its first voyage is part of its "fitting out," from adding the top decks and funnels to making sure the kitchens have enough pots and pans.

How long did it take to "fit out" the *Titanic*?

44 Ten months.

What did they install first?

45 The 29 boilers, the huge reciprocating engines, and the turbine.

The 15-foot (4.5-m)-high boilers

How did the engines work?

46 Coal was used to heat water in the boilers.

47 The boilers made high-pressure steam that ran the two reciprocating engines.

48 Those engines turned the two side propellers.

49 The leftover steam from the two engines ran a turbine that turned the center propeller.

50 The steam then ran to condensers that turned it back into water.

51 The pumps sent the condensed water back to the boilers.

How many lifeboats were originally planned?

52 The *Titanic*'s general manager, Alexander Carlisle, had 64 lifeboats in his original plans. The owners and builders reduced this number to 32 and finally to 16 because that was all the regulations required and because they wanted to make room for more deck space. Four lifeboats with collapsible canvas sides were added to bring the total to 20.

How much coal did the *Titanic* use?

53 The *Titanic* carried 5,892 tons (5,344 t) of coal. At a cruising speed of 21 to 22 knots, it used 620 to 640 tons (562 to 581 t) a day.

Why did the *Titanic* need masts?

54 The two 205-foot (62-m) masts did not have sails. They were used for a variety of purposes. The foremast at the front of the ship was fitted with a derrick that could lift cars and place them in one of the foreholds.

55 The foremast also had a ladder inside it to reach the crow's nest where the lookouts stood 90 feet (27 m) above the water.

56 Strung between the two masts were four wires, which relayed messages to and from the wireless room.

How were the propellers installed?

57 To do this, the *Titanic* was moved into a graving dock on February 3, 1912. This dock is an enclosed area where the water can be drained out so that work can be done on a ship's hull when it is in "dry dock."

How large were they?

58 The two three-bladed side propellers were each 23 ½ feet (7 m) across and weighed 38 tons (34 t) each.

59 The four-bladed center propeller was 16 ½ feet (5 m) wide and weighed 22 tons (20 t).

How large were the funnels?

64 Each of the four oval funnels averaged 63 feet (19 m) high, 19 feet (6 m) wide, and 24 ½ feet (7 m) long—big enough to drive two trains through.

Is it true the fourth funnel was a fake?

65 Yes. The *Titanic* and the *Olympic* needed only three funnels, but Lord Pirrie thought that a fourth funnel would make the ships look grander. The fourth funnel carried vents from the turbine engine room and from the huge coal stoves in the main kitchen.

How could there be electricity on a ship?

60 To run all the *Titanic*'s lights, machinery, and heating systems, there was a generating plant powered by steam from the boilers.

How much electrical cable was strung in the *Titanic*?

61 Two hundred miles (322 km).

How many portholes and windows were there?

62 About 2,000.

Were there telephones on board?

63 The *Titanic* had a 50-phone switchboard. The ship's crew could talk to one another on telephones located in the wheel house, forecastle, crow's nest, engine room, poop deck, chief engineer's cabin, engine room, stokeholds, and kitchen areas. Some of the first-class staterooms also had telephones. None of the phones could be used to talk to anyone on land.

GETTING READY

Crewmen peer out from the gash in the Olympic's hull *after the collision with the* Hawke. *Fortunately, no one on either ship was seriously injured.*

Is it true the *Olympic* had an accident before the *Titanic* even sailed?

66 Yes. On September 20, 1911, the *Olympic* collided with the British Royal Navy cruiser *Hawke*. The *Hawke* tore a 40-foot (12-m) gash in the liner's side. (Luckily, they managed to patch the hole so that the *Olympic* didn't sink.) But it made people wonder if these new superliners might be too big to navigate properly.

How did the *Olympic*'s accident affect the *Titanic*?

67 Shipyard workers had to stop work on the *Titanic* to repair her sister ship. This delayed the *Titanic*'s maiden voyage from March 20, 1912, to April 10, 1912.

Did they "test drive" the *Titanic*?

68 Just like a new car, a ship has to be tested before it can carry passengers and cargo. On April 2, 1912, tugs pulled the *Titanic* out to sea and her engines were fired up. The crew practiced port (left) and starboard (right) turns, stopping, turning a full circle, and running at different speeds. In all, her sea trials took less than a day.

Why were the sea trials so brief?

69 The *Titanic*'s short sea trials were enough to satisfy the builders and owners. Since the *Olympic* had performed well, it was assumed the *Titanic* would too. And the owners could not afford to have the *Titanic* miss its scheduled sailing day of April 10.

On the morning of April 2, 1912, the Titanic *heads for its sea trials.*

Was the captain on board for the sea trials?

70 Yes. Captain Edward John Smith and his officers participated in the trials on April 2. At 8:00 P.M. that same evening they guided the *Titanic* into the Irish Sea and headed for Southampton.

Where is Southampton?

71 Southampton is in the south of England on the River Test, which flows into the English Channel. It was easy for passengers to get there by train from London.

When did the *Titanic* arrive there?

72 Shortly after midnight on Thursday, April 4, 1912, the *Titanic* was tied up at Berth 44 at the White Star Dock.

How far had it traveled?

73 570 miles (917 km).

What happened to the *Titanic* on Good Friday, April 5?

74 As a salute to Southampton and its people, the ship was "dressed" in dozens of colorful flags and pennants.

Were people allowed on board to tour the new ship?

75 No. The ship was not quite finished. Painting and installing furniture, carpets, and fixtures still had to be completed before the ship sailed the following Wednesday.

What else had to be done before the ship could sail?

76 The hiring of most of the crew, including seamen, firemen, and stewards.

77 Filling the ship's huge bunkers with thousands of tons of coal.

78 "Provisioning" the ship with enough supplies to feed a small city.

79 Loading the cargo into the holds with 15 huge cranes and winches.

Why did a passenger ship carry general cargo?

80 Putting cargo on a passenger ship was the fastest way for a company to send its goods across the Atlantic. White Star could charge a lot of money for this service.

Why was the *Titanic* carrying dragon's blood?

81 Brown Brothers and Company shipped 76 cases of dragon's blood to the United States on the *Titanic*. Dragon's blood is the sap from a type of palm tree found in the Canary Islands. It was used to color wood varnish and women's makeup.

Was there really a car on board?

82 Yes. A new Renault was loaded into a forehold at Southampton.

What was the most exotic object in the *Titanic*'s cargo?

83 *The Rubaiyat of Omar Khayyam*, a book of ancient sayings. The illustrated copy in the *Titanic*'s hold was adorned with 1,050 precious stones, each set in gold. It had been recently sold for $2,025 (about $33,000 in today's dollars) at a London auction and was being sent to its new owner, Gabriel Wells, a New York book dealer.

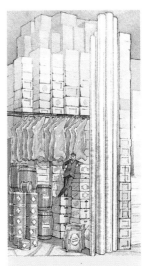

What are some examples of the *Titanic*'s general cargo?

Answers #84 – 97

- Ostrich plumes (12 cases)
- Shelled walnuts (300 cases)
- Sardines (25 cases)
- Straw hats (4 cases)
- Champagne (63 cases)
- Tennis balls (3 cases)
- Cheese (1 case)
- Velvet (1 case)
- Hair nets (4 packages)
- Potatoes (1,196 bags)
- Mercury (2 barrels)
- Olive oil (25 cases)
- Rough oak beams
- Grandfather clocks (2 cases)

THE TITANIC'S CREW

Who were the very first people to arrive at the docks on sailing day?

98 Just after sunrise at 5:18 A.M. on Wednesday, April 10, 1912, the first members of the crew began to board the *Titanic*. All of the officers except Captain Smith had already spent the night on board.

When did Captain Smith arrive?

99 At about 7:00 A.M. the captain said good-bye to his wife Eleanor and 12-year-old daughter Helen and took a taxi from his Southampton home to the White Star Dock. He climbed up the gangway at 7:30.

Is it true this was to be Captain Smith's last voyage?

100 At 62 years of age, after 38 years of service with White Star (25 years as a captain), Smith was due to retire at the end of the *Titanic*'s maiden voyage.

Why was he called the "Millionaire's Captain?"

101 The cheerful Captain Smith was well liked by the wealthy people who traveled on the White Star ships he commanded. Some even made a special point of reserving tickets on his ships.

What was his salary?

102 Captain Smith earned £1,250 ($6,250) a year plus a bonus of £200 ($1,000) if none of the ships he captained had an accident. (By comparison, the next in command, Chief Officer Henry Wilde, only earned £300/$1,500 a year.)

Captain Smith

Who were the *Titanic*'s officers?

Answers #103 – 109

The senior officers were:
- Chief Officer Henry Wilde
- First Officer William Murdoch
- Second Officer Charles Lightoller

The junior officers were:
- Third Officer Herbert Pitman
- Fourth Officer Joseph Boxhall
- Fifth Officer Harold Lowe
- Sixth Officer James Moody

What were their duties?

110 The officers managed the day-to-day activities of navigating the ship during their time on duty. They also had their own individual tasks to attend to: Wilde updated the ship's log; Boxhall updated the ship's charts; and Lowe and Moody were assigned to measure air and water temperatures every day.

How many crew members were on the *Titanic*?

111 Eight hundred and ninety-two were listed on the *Titanic*'s crew list.

What were their duties?

Answers #112 – 117

● **Seamen** assisted the officers in the day-to-day running of the ship.

● **Firemen** (also called stokers) shoveled the coal into the boilers.

● **Engineers** helped run the engines and machines.

● **Saloon stewards** set the tables, served food, and cleared tables in the dining rooms.

● **Bedroom stewards** (and stewardesses) served morning and afternoon tea, made beds, tidied staterooms, and cleaned the lounges and other public rooms.

● **Chefs** and their assistants prepared the meals.

How much were the crew paid?

118 The firemen could earn up to £72 ($360) per year, while stewardesses earned £42 ($210) each year.

What did the purser do?

Passengers line up outside a purser's office.

119 Purser H.W. McElroy's responsibilities included keeping the ship's accounts, processing the passengers' tickets, and managing personal requests related to their luggage and cargo. He was also in charge of the safe, and supervised two assistant pursers and four clerks.

Is it true there were teenage crew members?

120 Yes. Some were only 14 or 15 years old. They worked as bellboys (known as "buttons") carrying luggage, as pageboys running errands and delivering telegrams, or as "liftboys" running the elevators.

Two chefs prepare a meal (above), stokers shovel coal (far left), and a steward makes a bed (left).

How many women worked on the *Titanic*?

121 Twenty-three, including eighteen stewardesses, two cashiers, a masseuse, a Turkish Bath attendant, and a matron who acted as a chaperone for single women in third class. All but three were saved.

SAILING DAY

Who was the first passenger to come on board?

122 The ship's builder, Thomas Andrews, boarded at 6:00 A.M. He and nine other Harland & Wolff employees were on board to monitor the operation of the new ship.

Who else boarded early?

123 J. Bruce Ismay, the White Star managing director, arrived at 9:30 A.M. His room was an elegant parlor suite, which had a private promenade deck. In James Cameron's movie, Caledon Hockley had this same suite.

How did most of the passengers get to Southampton?

124 Trains, known as "boat trains," carried passengers from London's Waterloo Station right to the company's docks.

Thomas Andrews (inset) boarded the Titanic at Southampton's White Star Dock early on sailing day.

Did all of the passengers board the ship through the same entrance?

125 No. Each class had its own gangways. The first class entered on B-deck and D-deck, the second class on C-deck, and the third class on E-deck. (The *Titanic*'s decks were numbered alphabetically. The top deck was the boat deck, then came A-deck, B-deck, and so on downward.)

How much did it cost to buy a ticket on the *Titanic*?

Answers #126 – 130
● Ticket prices varied depending on the size and location of room chosen.

● A single first-class ticket averaged £86 ($430).
● The two deluxe parlor suites cost £660 ($3,300).

● Second-class tickets averaged £13 ($65).
● A third-class berth cost an average of £7 ($35).

WHITE STAR LINE.

YOUR ATTENTION IS SPECIALLY DIRECTED TO THE CONDITIONS OF TRANSPORTATION IN THE ENCLOSED CONTRACT. THE COMPANY'S LIABILITY FOR BAGGAGE IS STRICTLY LIMITED, BUT PASSENGERS CAN PROTECT THEMSELVES BY INSURANCE.

First Class Passenger Ticket per Steamship

SAILING FROM

Who greeted the first-class passengers when they came on board?

131 Chief Steward Latimer and his staff met them in the reception room as they came on board and escorted them to their staterooms. Male passengers were each given a flower for their buttonhole.

Who greeted the third-class passengers?

132 A medical officer. He wanted to be sure that none of the emigrants had any health problems that would prevent them from entering the United States.

Were third-class passengers escorted to their rooms?

133 No. Third-class tickets were stamped with a section number, but the berths were very hard to find. Stewards tried to direct the frustrated crowd, but many third-class passengers knew very little English and found it hard to follow the directions through the maze of halls and stairways.

What number wasn't used as a room number?

134 Thirteen.

Could passengers bring their dogs with them?

135 Yes. At least nine dogs were passengers on the *Titanic*.

What kinds of dogs were led up the gangways by their owners?

Answers #136 – 141
- A Pomeranian
- A Pekinese called Sun Yat Sen
- A chow chow
- An Airedale terrier named Kitty
- A champion French bulldog named Gamon de Pycombe
- A small dog named Frou Frou

Did any rich passengers bring their servants with them?

144 Yes. Thirty-one personal maids and valets came on the voyage.

Where were the dogs kept?

142 A lucky few stayed in their owners' staterooms while the others were locked up in the kennels.

Did passengers bring any other animals on the *Titanic*?

143 Marie Young, who had once taught piano to U.S. President Roosevelt's children, brought two prize French roosters and two hens with her. They were housed near the dog kennels and were cared for by the third-class butcher.

Where did the servants stay?

145 Most of the servants were given cabins beside or across from their employers so that they would be available to assist them during the voyage. They ate their meals in a dining room built just for them on C-deck.

146 Servants who weren't needed until docking, such as chauffeurs and cooks, were often berthed in second class.

Were there any bands playing or special ceremonies as the *Titanic* left Southampton?

147 Yes and no. The ship's own musicians played high up on the boat deck, but there were no special ceremonies. Crowds cheered from the docks, running alongside the colossal ship as it was slowly pulled toward the river. Excited passengers waved from the decks and windows as the *Titanic* blew its whistles and headed out to sea.

Did anyone miss the boat?

148 Seven stokers had gone ashore to visit one of the many pubs across from the dockyards. They stayed too long and by the time they rushed back to the *Titanic*, the gangway was being pulled up and new men had been hired to take their places.

GETTING SETTLED

Is it true that the rich had rooms on the top decks and the poor were down below?

149 Yes and no. It's true that only first-class rooms were on the upper A-, B-, and C-decks. But there were first-, second-, and third-class rooms on decks D and E. Decks F and G were second and third class only.

How many passengers were in each of the classes?

Answers #150 – 153

329 First-class passengers   **285** Second-class passengers   **710** Third-class passengers   **1,324** Total passengers

(These numbers are estimates, as no list is entirely accurate.)

How many children were in each class?

Answers #154 – 156

- First class = 5
- Second class = 22
- Third class = 76

Who were the richest children on board?

157 Probably eleven-year-old Billy Carter and his sister Lucile, who was fourteen. They were returning home to Philadelphia after a year in England, where their father had spent most of his time foxhunting while they were in boarding school.

What was their room like?

158 The Carters had a luxurious suite on B-deck with rooms nearby for their maid and valet. The new Renault stored in the *Titanic*'s hold was owned by Mr. Carter and their chauffeur was traveling in second class.

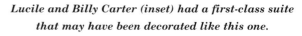

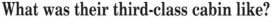
"OLYMPIC." First Class Suite Stateroom.

Lucile and Billy Carter (inset) had a first-class suite that may have been decorated like this one.

Which family was the largest on board?

A third-class cabin

159 The Sage family who were emigrating from Peterborough, England, to Jacksonville, Florida. It included parents John and Annie, and nine children between the ages of four and twenty.

What was their third-class cabin like?

160 The Sages probably needed two or even three cabins, although there were rooms on the *Titanic* in third class for up to ten people. Their rooms would have been simply furnished like the one shown on the left.

What did children like best about sleeping in third class?

161 The bunk beds!

Who was the youngest passenger?

162 Two-month-old Millvina Dean, who was traveling in third class with her parents and one-year-old brother, Bertram.

Did every room have its own washroom?

163 No. Although the *Titanic*'s toilet facilities were advanced for 1912, even some of the first-class passengers shared a washroom (right).

Where could you get a drink of water?

164 The washbasin taps in the rooms were connected to huge fresh water tanks in the bottom of the ship.

How many bathtubs were in third class?

165 Only two for more than 700 passengers!

A parlor suite

Where were the most luxurious rooms on the *Titanic*?

166 The two parlor suites with private promenade decks on B-deck were the most luxuriously decorated staterooms ever built on an ocean liner. The two other parlor suites were on C-deck. Each one had a sitting room, two bedrooms, two wardrobe rooms for clothes, and a private bathroom.

What was a typical first-class stateroom like?

167 A single-person room had a bed, large sofa, wardrobe, dressing table, and washbasin.

A first-class stateroom

What was a second-class cabin like?

168 Twelve-year-old Ruth Becker later remembered that their second-class cabin was "just like a hotel room, it was so big. Everything was new. New!" (Ruth had already traveled from India where her father was a missionary. Her one-year-old brother, Richard, had developed a serious illness and Ruth, her mother, and her younger sister were taking him to America's cooler climate.) The Beckers' cabin would have been like the one pictured above.

A second-class stateroom

After the passengers had unpacked, did they take their money and expensive jewelry to the purser's office?

169 Yes and no. Passengers seemed to keep their money with them. However, any items of great value were left with the purser, who kept them in his safe. At night, passengers could store watches or other valuables in a green mesh bag hanging on the wall next to their beds.

A BAD OMEN?

Is it true that the *Titanic* nearly collided with another ship when it was leaving Southampton?

170 Yes. As the *Titanic* moved down the narrow channel (**1**), it approached two ships, the *Oceanic* and the *New York* (**2**) moored together at the dock. The movement of the passing *Titanic* caused the *New York* to snap her mooring ropes and swing out toward the *Titanic* (**3**). As the *Titanic*'s passengers watched in horror, the *New York* began to swing ever closer toward them.

How close did the two ships come to colliding?

171 Only about 4 feet (1 m) separated them (see below).

What stopped them from hitting?

172 The order "Full astern!" was given and the sudden burst of water from the *Titanic*'s port propeller helped push the *New York* away.

173 The tugboats that were helping the liner leave the harbor attached lines to the *New York* to pull her away from the *Titanic* and moor her elsewhere (**4**).

How long did all this take?

174 Over an hour.

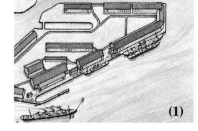

(1)

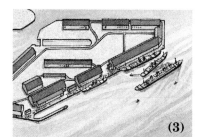

(2)

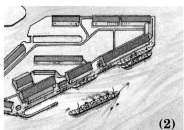

(3)

(4)

The stern of the New York *came very close to hitting the* Titanic.

What did the passengers think about the near collision?

175 Some people remarked that it was a bad omen for the start of a maiden voyage.

The tugboats belch smoke as they help move the Titanic *away from the pier.*

Were there any other problems that afternoon?

176 Yes. A fire was still burning in a coal bunker in boiler room No. 5. It had started several days earlier in Southampton.

Why wasn't the fire put out before the ship started its voyage?

177 The fire was burning very slowly and the chief engineer had assured Captain Smith that it wasn't a problem. Eight to ten stokers on each watch were assigned to water down the burning coal and to shovel it out of the bunker. Three days later the stubborn fire was extinguished.

Why was a bugle blown as soon as the *Titanic* was underway?

178 To announce that lunch was being served—over an hour later than planned because of the delayed departure.

What was served for the first lunch on the *Titanic*?

Answers #179 – 191

First-class diners were served:
● Garden soup
● Fillets of plaice (fish)
● Beef steak and kidney pie
● Roast Surrey capon (chicken)
● Grilled mutton chops
● Mashed, fried, and baked potatoes

A first-class luncheon menu

● Rice pudding, apples Manhattan, and pastries
● In addition, they could choose from a buffet that featured fresh lobsters, roast beef, Bologna sausage, galantine of chicken, and a selection of cheeses, as well as such delicacies as potted shrimps, soused herrings, sardines, and corned ox tongue!

Third-class passengers were served:
● Rice soup
● Corned beef and cabbage
● Boiled potatoes
● Cabin biscuits and bread
● Peaches and rice

Where was the *Titanic* headed?

192 Its first stop was Cherbourg, France, 67 miles (108 km) across the English Channel.

First Stop: CHERBOURG, FRANCE

How many passengers was the *Titanic* picking up in Cherbourg?

Answers #195 – 197
- 142 first-class
- 30 second-class
- 102 third-class

What disappointed the passengers?

198 After a six-hour train trip from Paris, they were told that the *Titanic* would be at least one hour late because of a near collision with another ship.

How long did it take the *Titanic* to get to Cherbourg?

193 More than four hours.

When did it arrive?

194 At 6:30 P.M., just as the sun was beginning to set.

How did the new passengers get out to the *Titanic*?

199 Two White Star tenders (small steamships), the *Nomadic* and the *Traffic*, had been built especially to carry Cherbourg passengers, luggage, and mail from the docks to the *Olympic* and the *Titanic*.

Off Cherbourg (top), the Nomadic (above) transported passengers and their luggage out to the waiting ship (below).

Why did the *Titanic* drop her anchor in the harbor rather than tying up at the docks?

200 Although Cherbourg was a deepwater port, it didn't have large enough docks for ships the size of the *Titanic*.

Were any of the new passengers rich or famous?

201 Yes! Some of the richest and best known of the *Titanic*'s passengers boarded in Cherbourg. Among them were:

202 John Jacob Astor, one of the world's richest men, aged 47 and estimated to be worth $150 million. He was returning home after an extended honeymoon with his new wife, 19-year-old Madeleine.

203 Benjamin Guggenheim, whose fortune came from his family's mining and smelting interests. He was traveling with a valet and chauffeur and a Madame Aubart, who was not his wife.

204 Margaret Tobin Brown, the colorful wife of a Denver mining magnate. After the sinking she would become known as the "Unsinkable Molly Brown."

Benjamin Guggenheim

205 Charlotte Cardeza and her 36-year-old son, Thomas, of Philadelphia, who had reserved one of the ultra-luxurious parlor suites with private promenade deck.

206 Sir Cosmo and Lady Duff Gordon. He was a Scottish aristocrat and sportsman. She was known as "Lucile" and was one of the most fashionable dress designers of her day. They were traveling as "Mr. and Mrs. Morgan," possibly because Lady Duff Gordon's fashion house had recently had problems with U.S. Customs.

Were other passengers traveling under false names?

Answers #207 – 209

● Yes, at least 15.

● One of these was Michel Navratil, who was going to America with his two young sons, Michel Jr. and Edmond. He was traveling under the name of Mr. Hoffman in an effort to fool his wife whom he had left in France.

● Another passenger, Alfred Nourney, grandly called himself "Baron von Drachstedt" and used his false name to get himself a first-class room with only a second-class ticket.

Did all classes travel together?

210 No. Only first- and second-class passengers were allowed on the *Nomadic*, which could handle up to 1,000 passengers and their luggage. The *Traffic* could carry up to 500 third-class passengers and bags of mail.

Who were the third-class passengers?

211 Mostly emigrants from Croatia, Armenia, Syria, and other middle-eastern countries.

Did any passengers get off at Cherbourg?

212 Yes. Fifteen first-class passengers and nine second-class passengers disembarked.

What unusual cargo was unloaded?

213 A canary belonging to a Mr. Meanwell. It cost him about 25¢ to take it across the Channel.

What time did the *Titanic* sail from Cherbourg?

214 After 90 minutes in the port, the *Titanic*'s crew pulled up the giant anchor and started up the engines. The brightly lit ship was underway by 8:10 P.M.

Next Stop:
QUEENSTOWN, IRELAND

The Titanic anchored off Queenstown on the morning of April 11, 1912.

On their way to Queenstown, what could Lucile and Billy Carter have for breakfast in first class?

Answers #215 – 226
● Baked apples
● Fresh fruit
● Several kinds of cereal
● Haddock and smoked salmon
● Grilled ham, sausage, and mutton
● Kidneys and bacon
● Vegetable stew
● Fried, shirred, poached, and boiled eggs
● Plain and tomato omelets
● Sirloin steak and mutton chops
● Mashed, sauteed, and jacket (baked) potatoes
● Scones, rolls, corn bread, and buckwheat cakes with jam, honey, or marmalade.

A first-class breakfast menu

What was on the second-class breakfast menu?

227 Twelve-year-old Ruth Becker's second-class menu was similar to the first-class one, but with fewer choices.

What was served for breakfast in third class?

Answers #228 – 232

Nine-year-old Frank Goldsmith, who was emigrating from England to Detroit with his parents, remembered being served
● Oatmeal porridge
● Smoked herring (a small fish)
● Jacket potatoes
● Tripe (part of a cow's or ox's stomach) and onions
● Swedish bread and marmalade

Yuck! Did people really eat this stuff?

233 People ate different foods back then than we do today. In years past, steerage passengers had to bring their own food for transatlantic voyages, so the third class on the *Titanic* probably considered themselves very lucky to be served this hearty food.

Why did the *Titanic* stop at Queenstown?

234 This small Irish port (known today as Cobh) was the traditional last stop for transatlantic ships. The *Titanic* picked up new passengers and let off those who were only going as far as Ireland. It also loaded and unloaded bags of mail.

Could the *Titanic* dock there?

235 No. Like Cherbourg, Queenstown didn't have a dock large enough to accommodate the *Titanic*, which had to anchor 2 miles (3 km) offshore.

What time did they arrive?

At 11:30 A.M. on Thursday, April 11.

Once the *Titanic* was at a standstill, what did the tenders *America* and *Ireland* carry out to her? *Answers #237 – 242*

- 113 third-class passengers, including many young Irish emigrants
- Seven second-class passengers
- Piles of luggage
- 1,385 sacks of mail
- Visiting press reporters and photographers
- Immigration officers

Who got off?

243 Seven passengers, including Francis M. Browne, a 32-year-old teacher who later became a Jesuit priest. His photographs of the voyage as far as Queenstown are among the few surviving from the *Titanic*.

How many people were now aboard the *Titanic*?

245 Approximately 2,207. Unfortunately, there is no exact record of everyone who was on board. Long before the age of computer technology, such lists were handwritten with copies prepared by several different people. With last-minute bookings and cancellations, in addition to those who missed the ship, it is impossible to determine exactly how many people were on the *Titanic*.

Why did someone hide in one of the tenders?

244 Twenty-eight-year-old stoker John Coffey probably signed on the *Titanic* to get a free ride home to Ireland. With the other firemen, he helped carry the mail to and from the tenders. When no one was looking, he hid under some bags of mail on one of the small boats and made his way to shore undetected.

A postcard of the two Queenstown tenders

What were the *Titanic*'s passengers doing while all of this activity was taking place?

246 Most had gone in to lunch, but some strolled along the decks or watched the tenders arrive. Others wandered down to the aft promenade deck where merchants from the Irish bumboats had set up a small market.

What are bumboats?

247 Bumboats are small boats used to carry provisions to ships anchored in a harbor. In Queenstown, they carried sellers of Irish lace, china, and other souvenirs out to the *Titanic*.

What did John Jacob Astor buy for his young wife?

248 It's said that the wealthy American bought a beautiful lace shawl for his pregnant wife, Madeleine. He apparently paid £165 ($825) for it, a very large sum of money in those days.

As the *Titanic* was steaming away from Queenstown, what did the passengers hear?

249 At 1:55 P.M. the *Titanic* gave three long, mournful blasts on her whistle. A tender honked a reply, and the liner gave a final, short blast.

250 Down on the third-class promenade deck, Eugene Daly said good-bye to his native country by playing a sad song, "Erin's Lament," on his Irish bagpipes.

What time did they leave?

At 1:40 P.M. on Thursday, April 11.

Exploring
THE SHIP *of* DREAMS

What room was the grandest of all on the *Titanic*?

252 The first-class lounge was decorated to look like a room from the palace of Versailles. It had elaborately carved paneling and a marble fireplace on which stood a classical statue called the "Artemis of Versailles."

What room was the most fantastic?

253 The cooling room where passengers relaxed after a Turkish steam bath. It was decorated to look like a room in a sultan's palace with richly colored tiles, gilded beams, and bronze lights (below).

Passengers dressed for dinner meet on the elegant Grand Staircase.

How grand was the Grand Staircase?

254 Very. The natural light that shone through the wrought-iron and glass dome reflected off the oak wall paneling and the gilt of the elaborate stair railings. On the top landing a large carved panel contained a clock surrounded by two classical figures, symbolizing Honor and Glory Crowning Time. The staircase went all the way from the boat deck down to the reception room outside the dining saloon on D-deck, and then continued down to E-deck.

Was there another Grand Staircase?

255 Yes. There was a more modest version of the staircase, topped by a smaller glass dome, farther back in the ship.

Is it true that some rooms were reserved for men only?

256 Yes. The three smoking rooms were male-only preserves. It was not considered proper for women to smoke in public in 1912.

The first-class smoking room

Did one of them look like a fancy men's club?

257 Yes. The first-class smoking room had stained-glass windows and mahogany paneling inlaid with mother-of-pearl. Green leather chairs were grouped around small tables that had raised edges to prevent glasses from sliding off when the sea was rough. The second-class smoking room was less grand, but also had a clubby atmosphere.

Was there a room for women only?

258 Yes and no. The first-class reading and writing room was intended as a retreat where women could read and write letters. It was decorated with white walls and delicate furniture. Men could use it, but few did.

Was there a ballroom?

259 No. There was no organized dancing on the *Titanic*.

Could you shop on board?

260 Not really. But the two barbershops sold postcards, small gifts, and souvenirs such as White Star pennants and paperweights.

Could you get your laundry done?

261 No. The ship's laundry (sheets and towels) was washed in port. But you could give your clothes to a bedroom steward for ironing. A small fee applied.

What if you got sick?

262 There was a hospital on D-deck and two doctors on board.

Could the classes mix?

263 No. Second-class passengers could tour the first-class public rooms before sailing but after that had to stay in the second-class areas. Third-class passengers were restricted to third-class areas and the poop deck.

Why was it called the poop deck?

264 A poop deck is the highest outdoor deck on a ship's stern. This word can be traced to the Latin word "puppis," which means the end section of a ship.

Why was third class called "steerage"?

265 This term referred to the cheapest possible ticket. Historically, the "steerage" was the stern area of a ship near the rudder, or steering equipment. It was the least expensive place to stay on board because it was the most uncomfortable.

WHAT DID *the* PASSENGERS DO *for* FUN?

Riding the mechanical horse in the gym

What did children do for fun on the *Titanic*?

Answers #266 – 272

Children in first class could:
● Ride a mechanical horse or camel in the gymnasium or use a stationary bicycle or rowing machine. The gymnasium was reserved for children between 1:00 and 3:00 P.M. every day. The gym instructor, T.W. McCawley, enjoyed showing them how to use the equipment.
● Watch the passengers' dogs being walked by a steward every morning and afternoon on the poop deck.
● Play deck quoits, shuffleboard, or other games. Six-year-old Douglas Spedden of Tuxedo Park, New York, played with his spinning top on the boat deck.
● Attend a concert in the first-class lounge in the evenings.

Children in second class:
● Skipped and played games like "horse racing" on deck, according to a surviving passenger, Selena Rogers Cook. Ruth Becker pushed her brother Richard about the decks in a White Star Line stroller.
● Read books in the library.

Douglas Spedden spins his top.

Children in third class:
● Played games on the poop deck. Frank Goldsmith remembered swinging on the huge baggage cranes in the well deck and getting his hands covered with oily grease. He and a group of friends he met on board ran up and down stairs exploring every part of the ship open to third-class children. They even looked down into the boiler rooms and waved at the stokers shoveling coal.

What did adults do for fun on the *Titanic*?

Answers #273 – 286

First-class passengers:
● Went swimming in the pool for a cost of 25¢ per ticket. It was filled with sea water. The *Olympic* and *Titanic* were among the first liners to have a pool on board. Men could swim free of charge between 6:00 and 9:00 in the morning.
● Played squash in the court on G-deck. Tickets

In the gymnasium, passengers enjoyed the latest exercise machines.

were 50¢ and included the services of the ship's professional, Fred Wright.
● Exercised in the gymnasium.
● Relaxed in the Turkish Baths. These were reserved for women from 10:00 A.M. to 1:00 P.M. and for men from 2:00 P.M. to 6:00 P.M.
● Played cards, read, and socialized in the lounge or the smoking room.
● Lay in deck chairs covered in White Star blankets while stewards brought them hot drinks. Chairs and blankets could be rented for the voyage at a cost of $1 each.
● Met friends before meals in the reception room.
● Sent messages to friends from the middle of the ocean through the wireless room.
● Took photographs and developed them in the darkroom on A-deck.

Second-class passengers:
● Read, played cards, or socialized in the second-class library or smoking room. Chess, dominoes, and other games were also available.
● Walked and used deck chairs on the decks reserved for second class.

The first-class promenade

Third-class passengers:
● Met friends in the third-class lounge known as the "general room" or smoked and played cards in the "smoke room."
● Some passengers played instruments and danced on deck or in the general room.
● Walked and sat on benches on the poop deck, which was for third-class use.

Was there gambling?

287 Yes. There were three professional "cardsharps" on board (traveling under false names) who played cards for money. There was also a daily betting pool on how far the ship had traveled each day.

Was there an orchestra on board?

288 Yes. The eight musicians hired for the trip played in two small string groups. A quintet, led by violinist Wallace Hartley, held concerts for first-class passengers. A trio played in the reception room outside the à la carte restaurant.

Is it true the *Titanic* had its own newspaper?

289 Yes. A daily newspaper called the *Atlantic Daily Bulletin* was prepared aboard ship. In addition to news articles and advertisements, it contained a daily menu, the latest stock prices, horse-racing results, and society gossip.

What did the passengers on the *Titanic* enjoy the most?

290 The meals!

EATING ON BOARD

When were the passengers served their meals?

Answers #291 – 293

- Breakfast, 8:30 to 10:30 A.M.
- Lunch, 1:00 to 2:30 P.M.
- Dinner, 6:00 to 7:30 P.M.

Where did the first-class passengers eat their meals?

294 In the first-class dining saloon. This impressive dining room was the largest room on any ship of the day. It was 114 feet (35 m) long and 92 feet (28 m) wide and had an elaborate molded plaster ceiling and leaded-glass windows. It could seat over 550 people at a time.

Passengers enjoyed 11-course dinners in the spacious first-class dining saloon. At each course, waiters circulated with silver serving platters.

Where was the most elegant place to eat?

295 The beautiful à la carte restaurant served lavish food to the *Titanic*'s wealthiest passengers.

What was the Café Parisien?

296 The Café Parisien (below) looked like a real sidewalk café in Paris. Passengers would go there after dinner or between meals to sip coffee or eat elegant little sandwiches served by the café's French waiters.

What song did the bugler play to announce that lunch and dinner were ready?

297 "The Roast Beef of Old England," a traditional tune.

Could Ruth Becker and Frank Goldsmith go to the restaurant or café?

298 No. The second- and third-class passengers ate in their own dining saloons.

Why were the dining rooms called "saloons"?

299 The word "saloon" comes from the French word "salon," which means a spacious and elegant room where important people would meet.

How much food did the *Titanic* carry?

Although the *Titanic*'s provisioning list has been lost, the *Olympic*'s lists give us a good idea of what its sister ship carried. Here are some examples:

Answers #300 – 324

- **Fresh meat**
  75,000 pounds
  (34,000 kg)
- **Fresh fish**
  11,000 pounds
  (5,000 kg)
- **Bacon and ham**
  7,500 pounds
  (3,400 kg)
- **Fresh eggs**
  40,000
- **Sausages**
  2,500 pounds
  (1,100 kg)
- **Sweetbreads**
  (calves' organs)
  1,000

- **Coffee**
  2,200 pounds
  (1,000 kg)
- **Tea**
  800 pounds
  (360 kg)
- **Sugar**
  10,000 pounds
  (4,500 kg)
- **Flour**
  200 barrels
- **Grapes**
  1,000 pounds
  (450 kg)
- **Oranges**
  36,000

- **Lemons**
  16,000
- **Fresh milk**
  1,500 gallons
  (5,700 L)
- **Fresh cream**
  1,200 quarts
  (1,300 L)
- **Fresh butter**
  6,000 pounds
  (2,700 kg)
- **Grapefruit**
  50 boxes
- **Lettuce**
  7,000 heads
- **Tomatoes**
  2 ¾ tons (2 t)

- **Fresh asparagus**
  800 bundles
- **Fresh green peas**
  2,250 pounds
  (1,020 kg)
- **Onions**
  3,500 pounds
  (1,600 kg)
- **Potatoes**
  40 tons (35 t)
- **Jams and**
  marmalades
  1,120 pounds
  (500 kg)
- **Ice cream**
  1,750 quarts
  (1,990 L)

Did the orchestra play during meals?

325 Yes. The quintet performed in both the first- and second-class dining saloons.

Could you get breakfast in bed?

326 Not really. The stewards brought first-class passengers morning tea, which could include scones, toast, or fruit. But the full breakfast menu was available only in the dining saloon.

How many chefs and chefs' assistants worked in the *Titanic*'s five kitchens?

Cooks prepared over 6,000 meals each day.

327 Sixty — from soup cooks and roast cooks to pastry cooks and vegetable cooks. There was a kosher cook, too, to prepare the meals for the Jewish passengers.

Who set the tables in the dining saloons?

328 Saloon stewards set the tables, served the food, and cleared away the dishes after every meal. They worked very long hours, from 6:00 A.M. until 9:00 P.M., with a one-hour break in the afternoon.

Who washed the dishes?

329 Thirty-six glassmen, plate-washers, and scullerymen.

Where did they throw out the garbage?

330 Food scraps were tossed overboard and eaten by seabirds and fish.

THE TITANIC'S PASSENGERS

What countries did the passengers come from?

331 Most of the passengers on board the *Titanic* came from Great Britain (which then included Ireland) and the United States. There were also quite a few people from Canada, Finland, Norway, Sweden, and Syria. Other countries represented included: Argentina, Armenia, Australia, Austria, Belgium, Bulgaria, China, Croatia, Denmark, France, Greece, India, Italy, Japan, Lebanon, Mexico, the Netherlands, Peru, Portugal, Russia, South Africa, Switzerland, Thailand, Turkey, and Uruguay.

How many Canadians were there?

332 Approximately 50, of whom only 15 were saved.

333 The richest Canadian was Harry Molson, a member of the beer-brewing family and president of Molson's Bank in Montreal.

334 The most prominent Canadian was Charles Hays, president of the Grand Trunk Railway, who was returning for the opening of his company's new hotel in Ottawa, the Chateau Laurier.

Were there any well-known British passengers?

Answers #335 – 339

●The Countess of Rothes, on her way to meet her husband in North America.

●William T. Stead, an influential London journalist.

●Sir Cosmo Duff Gordon and his wife, Lucile, a dress designer (see p. 25).

●Thomas Pears, heir to the Pears soap fortune.

●Hugh Woolner, son of a famous sculptor.

Lady Duff Gordon

Were there any movie stars?

340 Yes, one, Dorothy Gibson, a 28-year-old silent screen actress. She would later star in *Saved from the Titanic*, a movie made one month after the disaster. Her costume was the dress she wore on the night of the sinking.

Were any passengers on their honeymoons?

341 Thirteen couples traveling on the *Titanic* were on their honeymoons, eight in first class.

Is it true that there was a murderer on the ship?

342 Yes. Alice Cleaver had been convicted of murdering her own baby three years before the *Titanic* sailed. Once released from jail, Alice hoped to begin a new life in Canada. Concealing her crime, she managed to get herself hired by Montrealers Hudson and Bess Allison as a nanny for their two small children, Loraine and Trevor.

Alice Cleaver with Trevor Allison

Were there many wealthy people on board?

343 Yes. In addition to John Jacob Astor and Benjamin Guggenheim (see p. 25), there was Isidor Straus, who had built up his $50 million fortune as co-owner of Macy's department store in New York City. Other rich passengers on the *Titanic* included J. Bruce Ismay, George Dunton Widener, Charles Melville Hays, William Dulles, Harry Molson, Emil Taussig, Frederick Maxfield Hoyt, Clarence Moore, John Borland Thayer, and the "Unsinkable" Molly Brown.

Wealthy first-class passengers included John Jacob and Madeleine Astor (left), the "Unsinkable" Molly Brown (right), and Isidor and Ida Straus (inset left). George Widener (inset right) was heir to the largest fortune in Philadelphia.

How much were they worth?

344 All of the wealthy first-class passengers together were said to be worth $600 million ($9.8 billion in today's money).

How did passengers find out who was on board?

345 A booklet containing the names of first- and second-class passengers was printed and distributed in the staterooms.

Did people have premonitions about the *Titanic*?

Answers #346 – 348

● Chief Officer Wilde wrote in a letter to his sister from the ship: "I still don't like this ship. I have a queer feeling about it."

● Survivor Eva Hart, who was seven in 1912, later claimed that her mother sat up every night rather than go to sleep on the *Titanic* because she was afraid there would be an accident.

● Some relatives of *Titanic* passengers claimed to have had feelings of doom about the ship and to have woken up at the time of the sinking with visions of people drowning.

WARNINGS OF DISASTER

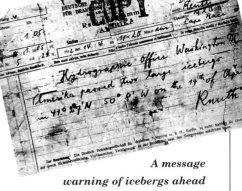

A message warning of icebergs ahead

How many miles did the *Titanic* cover on Friday, April 12?

349 Three hundred and eighty-six nautical miles (715 km) since midday on Thursday.

How many on Saturday, April 13?

350 Five hundred and nineteen nautical miles (961 km).

Was it trying for a speed record?

351 No. The *Titanic* would never be as fast as a ship like the *Mauretania*, which had a top speed of 26 knots. But it may have been trying to surpass the number of miles covered each day by the *Olympic* on its maiden voyage.

When did the *Titanic* first receive a warning of ice ahead?

352 On Friday, April 12, several eastbound ships sent messages congratulating the *Titanic* on its maiden voyage. They also mentioned that ice was in the sea-lanes.

How did a ship receive messages in 1912?

353 The wireless operators on the *Titanic* received and sent messages by radio waves using Morse code. With a small key, they tapped out dots and dashes representing the letters of the alphabet and numbers zero through nine. These signals were picked up by other ships or by wireless stations on land.

What did Captain Smith do when warned of ice ahead?

354 He steered farther south. Ice in the sea-lanes was not uncommon during April. Icebergs and sea ice from Greenland float south each spring past the Grand Banks, off Newfoundland. Normal navigational practice was to steer around icebergs once they had been sighted by the lookouts. To avoid the ice, westbound ships also took a route farther south than usual to a location called "the corner." Once there, they headed straight west.

Where did the *Titanic*'s wireless operators work and sleep?

355 Twenty-five-year-old Jack Phillips, the first wireless operator, and his 22-year-old assistant, Harold Bride, worked in a small windowless room on the forward boat deck. To make sure that the ship's wireless room was operating 24 hours a day, the men took turns sleeping on the bunks in the tiny room next door.

Were they part of the ship's crew?

356 No. They worked for the Marconi Company. Their primary job was to send and receive messages paid for by the passengers.

A ship's wireless operator taps out a message.

How much did they earn a year?

357 Phillips earned £51 ($255) a year; Bride was paid £25.50 ($127.50) a year.

Were there many messages sent and received on the *Titanic*?

358 Yes. Phillips and Bride were kept very busy. Passengers loved to send greetings to their friends and relatives from an ocean liner, particularly a famous one on its maiden voyage.

How much did it cost to send a wireless message?

359 Most messages cost $3 for the first ten words and 35¢ for each additional one.

What upset both Phillips and Bride late Saturday night?

360 The wireless machine stopped working at about 11:00 P.M. Both men worked through the night until the problem was discovered and repaired at 5:00 A.M. on Sunday.

What was on the bridge of the *Titanic*?

361 The bridge was the enclosed area at the front of the top deck from which the ship was navigated. It contained instruments such as a compass, used for determining the ship's direction; brass telegraphs, which gave orders to the engine rooms; and the telemotor connected to the ship's main steering wheel.

Who worked on the bridge?

362 Captain Smith, the officers, and the quartermasters. Each day on the *Titanic* was divided into six watches of four hours each. The officers worked in shifts (four hours on, followed by eight hours off) navigating the ship.

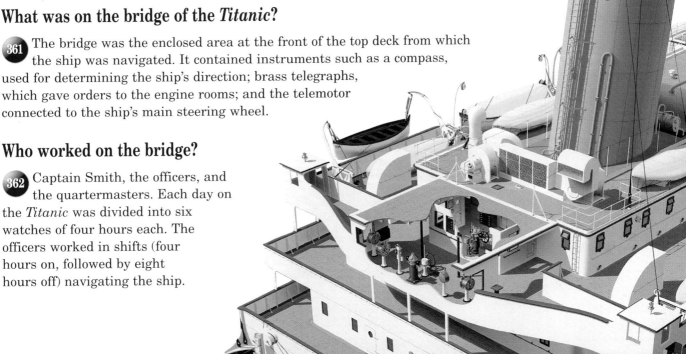

A PEACEFUL SUNDAY

Did more iceberg warnings arrive on Sunday, April 14?

363 Yes. At 9:00 A.M. the eastbound liner *Caronia* reported "bergs, growlers and field ice in 42° N, from 49° to 51° W." Captain Smith posted the message on the bridge for his officers to read.

364 At 11:40 A.M. the Dutch liner *Noordam* reported "much ice" in about the same place.

What's a growler?

365 Growlers are dark-colored slabs of ice that have broken away from the ice pack or from icebergs.

What did the passengers do that morning?

366 Colonel Archibald Gracie, a military historian, played a pre-breakfast game of squash with the ship's pro, Fred Wright. He then took a dip in the pool. After a large breakfast, the colonel attended a church service along with many of his fellow passengers.

Where were the services held?

367 A service for first-class passengers was led by Captain Smith in the first-class dining saloon at 11:00 A.M.

368 Reginald Barker, the assistant purser, led a Church of England service in the second-class dining saloon. Eva Hart was thrilled when one of her favorite hymns, "O God Our Help in Ages Past," was sung.

369 Father Thomas Byles conducted a Catholic Mass in the second-class lounge, followed by one for third class.

Was there a lifeboat drill on Sunday?

370 It is believed that the usual Sunday lifeboat drill was canceled because of the strong breeze, and perhaps so as not to alarm the passengers. One crew member later testified that such drills were only conducted while docked in New York, because they were not compulsory under British law.

Why did the passengers gather at the purser's office at noon?

371 Each day the officers used sextants aimed at the sun to determine the *Titanic*'s position. They then posted the daily distance record. On Sunday it read, "Since noon, Saturday, 546 miles." The passengers noted that this was the best record so far.

How fast was the *Titanic* going on Sunday?

372 Two more boilers had been lit that morning. By late afternoon, the ship was traveling at around 22 knots, almost full speed.

Was anyone on board celebrating a birthday that day?

373 Alfred Rush, who was traveling to America with Frank Goldsmith's family, turned 16 that day and was proudly wearing a new pair of long trousers. (Boys under 16 wore short pants in 1912.)

Did any more iceberg warnings arrive that afternoon?

374 The wireless room picked up two more. One at 1:42 P.M. from the White Star Liner *Baltic* reported icebergs and field ice about 250 miles (400 km) in front of the *Titanic*. Three minutes later the German liner *Amerika* reported that it had passed two large bergs and asked the *Titanic* to relay the message to the United States Hydrographic Office. The first message was delivered to Captain Smith, the second wasn't, apparently because it wasn't addressed to the captain.

What did Captain Smith do with the *Baltic*'s warning?

375 Intending to show it to his officers later, Captain Smith took the *Baltic*'s message down to lunch with him. On his way, he ran into J. Bruce Ismay and gave him the ice warning because he thought it might interest him.

What did Ismay do with the telegram?

376 Late that afternoon, Ismay came across two wealthy Philadelphia ladies, Emily Ryerson and Marian Thayer, who were watching the sunset from deck chairs. "We are in among the icebergs," he announced, pulling the telegram out of his pocket. He didn't seem at all worried and told the women that the ship would probably reach New York ahead of schedule.

What did people do before dinner?

378 Some passengers spent the afternoon writing letters, curled up with a book, visiting friends, or playing cards. A few put on warm clothes to see the beautiful sunset on deck.

379 Helen Candee, an author, and Hugh Woolner rode the mechanical horses and stationary bicycles in the gymnasium and then relaxed on a green velvet settee in front of the first-class lounge's fireplace. Stewards served them hot tea and buttered toast.

380 Ruth Becker once again pushed her brother Richard in a stroller along the enclosed promenade deck, watched by the Navratil brothers who were there playing with their father.

381 In third class, some of the passengers began dancing in the general room (where Jack and Rose danced in the movie). A few off-duty crew members joined the fun.

Why did most passengers stay inside that afternoon?

377 The temperature began to drop after lunch. By 7:30 P.M., it was a chilly 33°F (0.6°C).

Did the *Titanic* slow down later that afternoon as it approached the ice reported by the *Baltic*?

382 No. Captain Smith did alter the ship's course so that it would make the turn at "the corner" 10 miles (16 km) farther south than usual. The bridge officers thought this was a precaution to avoid the ice.

THE LAST EVENING

Where was Captain Smith on the *Titanic*'s last evening?

383 He went to a dinner party in the à la carte restaurant. It was hosted by wealthy Philadelphians George and Eleanor Widener and attended by their 27-year-old son Harry; their Philadelphia friends, John and Marian Thayer and William and Lucile Carter; and Major Archibald Butt, an aide to U.S. President Taft. The restaurant's chef had prepared a special menu for the meal, featuring expensive food and wine.

Captain Smith dines with first-class passengers in the 1958 movie A Night to Remember *(above). Third-class passengers relax in the general room (right).*

Were any children invited?

384 No. Lucile and Billy Carter probably ate in their family's stateroom.

385 The Thayers' 17-year-old son Jack had his dinner alone in the dining saloon. Over coffee he made a new friend, 29-year-old Milton Long, who impressed Jack with stories of his travels.

What did the first-class passengers do after dinner?

386 The orchestra played in the reception room outside the dining saloon. Passengers had coffee there or in the lounge. Several card games began in the crowded smoking room and continued well after most of the other passengers had gone to bed.

What did the second-class passengers do after dinner?

387 Reverend Ernest C. Carter, a London vicar, led nearly 100 passengers in a hymn-sing. One passenger remembered singing the hymn that ends with *"O hear us when we cry to Thee for those in peril on the sea."*

What did the third-class passengers do that night?

388 Another party with music began in the general room.

A rat ran across the floor and several girls squealed while their young admirers chased it. At 10:00 P.M. the crew turned out the lights in the public rooms and the third-class passengers went to bed.

Were there any more iceberg warnings that evening?

389 At 7:30 P.M., Harold Bride overheard a warning — this time from the *Californian* — reporting three large icebergs. Bride delivered the message to the bridge, but it wasn't posted or passed on to Captain Smith. The ice now lay only 50 miles (80 km) ahead of the *Titanic*.

How did the officers prepare for the ice ahead?

390 After Second Officer Lightoller came on duty at 6:00 P.M., he asked Sixth Officer Moody to calculate when they would reach the ice, using the *Caronia*'s position as a guide. Moody later told him that the ship would encounter it around 11:00 P.M. that evening.

391 At 7:15 P.M. First Officer Murdoch asked the lamp trimmer, Samuel Hemming, to close a hatch on the forward deck as there was a glow coming from it. Any light would make it harder to see an iceberg.

392 At 9:30 P.M. Lightoller asked the two lookouts in the crow's nest to "keep a sharp lookout for ice, particularly small ice and growlers."

Did Captain Smith return to the bridge?

393 After saying good-night to the Wideners and their dinner guests, he visited the bridge at 8:55 P.M. He and Lightoller talked about whether icebergs would be visible on such a calm, clear night. At 9:20 P.M. Captain Smith left for his cabin nearby, saying, "If it becomes at all doubtful let me know at once. I shall be just inside."

Second Officer Lightoller

Sixth Officer Moody

Jack Phillips

Harold Bride

Did Captain Smith order Lightoller to reduce speed?

394 No. The captain said that if it became hazy they would have to slow down, but until it did, he no doubt believed that the lookouts would see any ice in plenty of time to steer around it.

Is it true an important ice warning was not delivered to the bridge?

395 Yes. A telegram arrived at about 9:30 P.M. from the steamer *Mesaba* warning of heavy pack ice and large icebergs. But Jack Phillips put it aside and continued transmitting a backlog of passengers' messages. After all, three ice warnings had already been delivered to the bridge. What Phillips didn't know was that only one of them had been posted.

Were the lookouts watching for icebergs?

396 At 10:00 P.M. Lightoller finished his watch and was relieved on the bridge by Murdoch. The two lookouts, Archie Jewell and George Symons, were relieved by Frederick Fleet and Reginald Lee, who were also told to watch out for small ice and growlers.

Did Jack Phillips really say "Shut up!" to the last ice warning?

397 Yes. The captain of the *Californian* had stopped his ship for the night in the middle of the ice field. He asked his wireless operator to warn other ships of the danger. The tired Phillips curtly cut off the *Californian*'s operator at around 10:55 P.M. The fatal iceberg lay 45 minutes away.

ICEBERG RIGHT AHEAD!

Can you smell icebergs before you see them?

398 Yes. Lookout Archie Jewell had told his mate George Symons, "You can smell the ice before you get to it." Passenger Elizabeth Shutes recalled that the air that evening smelled strange, like the ice cave in Switzerland's Eiger Glacier. Icebergs break off from glaciers in Greenland. The minerals in them give off a distinctive odor as the icebergs melt on their journey south.

When did the lookout see the iceberg?

399 At 11:39 P.M.

Why didn't the lookouts see the iceberg sooner? *Answers #400 – 402*

● It was a cold, clear night and the sea was calm. This meant that there were no waves to make a white ring of foam as they broke around the iceberg's base.

● There was no moon to reflect off the berg.
● The lookouts had to rely on their own eyesight because they thought the binoculars had been left in Southampton.

What happened when they saw the iceberg?

403 Lookout Frederick Fleet rang the warning bell three times and telephoned the bridge: "Iceberg right ahead!"

404 First Officer Murdoch ran to the ship's telegraph and sent an order to the engine room: "Stop! Full speed astern!" He wanted the *Titanic*'s engines to be stopped, then reversed.

405 At the same time, he called to Quartermaster Robert Hichens at the wheel: "Hard a'starboard!" Murdoch then pressed a button that rang an alarm down in the engine room, and flipped the switch that closed the doors between the watertight compartments.

(1)

(2)

The **Titanic** *turns slowly (1), but seconds later, it hits the iceberg (2), which scrapes along its starboard bow (3).*

(3)

Did the ship turn?

406 While the officers on the bridge held their breath, the ship kept going straight toward the berg. Then slowly, slowly, the *Titanic* began to turn. But it was too late. The officers felt a slight jolt, and then heard a grinding sound from far below, on the starboard side.

How many seconds passed between Fleet's warning to the bridge and the moment of impact?

407 Thirty-seven seconds.

How big was the iceberg that the *Titanic* hit?

408 Eyewitnesses reported that the iceberg was just higher than the boat deck, which meant that it was over 60 feet (18 m) high.

Did any of the passengers see the iceberg?

409 Yes. First-class passenger Henry Sleeper Harper sat up in bed and saw the iceberg scrape against his window.

410 Billy and Lucile Carter's father was in the smoking room when he felt a jolt and heard a strange grinding noise. Mr. Carter and a few of the men ran out on deck in time to see a dark shape against the starlit sky.

Who saw the damage first?

411 Stokers in boiler room No. 6, the one closest to the bow, had just received the "Stop!" order when icy water suddenly poured through a gash in the hull. The men ran for their lives as the watertight door between their compartment and the next began to come down. Two men were able to slide under the door before it shut, while the third had to scramble up an emergency ladder.

When did Captain Smith find out?

412 Right away. He rushed into the wheelhouse from his cabin and asked, "What have we struck?" Murdoch replied, "An iceberg, sir." Smith asked if the watertight doors had been closed and was told they had. He and Murdoch then walked quickly to the starboard wing of the bridge looking for the iceberg, but it was gone.

What did he do next?

413 Smith ordered Fourth Officer Boxhall to inspect the ship for damage.

By stopping and reversing the engines, had Murdoch made the collision a certainty?

414 Yes. The faster a ship is going forward, the faster it can turn. If the *Titanic* had turned just a little more, it would have missed the iceberg entirely.

Would it have been better if the *Titanic* had hit the iceberg straight on?

415 Yes. Most people think that if the ship's bow had crashed straight into the iceberg, the *Titanic* and most of its passengers would have survived. If only a small part of the bow had hit the iceberg, much less water would have entered the ship. With its watertight compartments closed, the *Titanic* might have stayed afloat until help arrived.

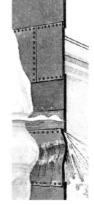

Did the iceberg cut a gash in the hull?

416 For years it was thought that the iceberg had sliced a 300-foot (92-m)-long gash in the *Titanic*'s hull. But when Dr. Robert Ballard dived to the wreck and examined the hull in 1986, he noticed that the riveted plates of the hull had been scraped and bumped, not sliced, and that the rivets holding them together had popped open, allowing water to rush in.

WE'VE STRUCK AN ICEBERG!

Did any ice break off and land on the ship?

423 Yes. When Jack Thayer and his father went out on the first-class deck to find out why the engines had stopped, they noticed some boys on a lower deck playing with chunks of ice.

What did it feel like when the *Titanic* hit the iceberg?

Answers #417 – 422

● Some of the third-class passengers sleeping just above the cargo holds in the bow were knocked out of their beds and heard a "tremendous noise."

● Many first- and second-class passengers felt only a "faint grinding jar" or nothing at all.

● Jack Thayer was just climbing into bed when the ship seemed to sway slightly.

● Walter Belford, the chief night baker, also felt a slight swaying motion that sent a pan of freshly baked rolls clattering to the floor.

● Frank Goldsmith's father and Ruth Becker's mother woke up when the engines stopped, unused to the silence.

● Builder Thomas Andrews was in his cabin poring over the ship's plans and considering possible improvements. He didn't notice the collision.

What did Joseph Boxhall find?

424 During a 15-minute inspection tour, Fourth Officer Boxhall saw no damage as low as F-deck. He reported this to the captain who told him to find the ship's carpenter and "sound" the ship (check it for damage). Leaving the bridge, Boxhall saw the carpenter who told him the ship was taking in water fast. He then met a mail clerk who told him, "The mail hold is filling rapidly!" With these reports, Captain Smith summoned the ship's builder, Thomas Andrews, and they made a quick tour of the damaged areas.

What did Captain Smith and Thomas Andrews discover?

425 Water was pouring into the mail room on G-deck, where five postal clerks were desperately trying to drag 200 sacks of mail up to F-deck. Ten minutes after the collision, the first five compartments of the hull were filling and the water's weight was already pulling the bow down.

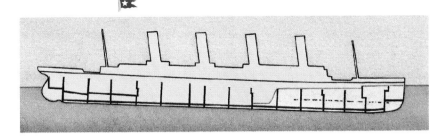

With six of its sixteen compartments flooded, the Titanic *could not survive.*

Why didn't the "watertight" compartments work?

426 The first six of the sixteen compartments had been opened by the iceberg. The *Titanic* could float with the first four compartments flooded, but not any more than that. The bulkheads—the walls between the compartments—rose only 10 feet (3 m) above the waterline. As each compartment filled and the bow sank lower, the water would slosh over into the next one.

When did J. Bruce Ismay hear the news?

427 The White Star Line managing director had been awakened in his suite by a scraping noise. He thought the ship might have dropped a propeller blade. Throwing an overcoat over his pajamas, he headed for the bridge. Captain Smith told him what had happened. "Do you think the ship is seriously damaged?" Ismay asked. "I am afraid she is," the captain replied.

Why couldn't they pump the water out?

428 Engineers and firemen quickly rigged hoses to the bilge pumps in an attempt to keep the rising water under control. But they couldn't keep up and were forced to abandon their efforts when the bulkhead between boiler rooms No. 5 and 6 collapsed.

When did Captain Smith order Chief Officer Wilde to uncover the lifeboats?

429 At 12:05 A.M., after his conversation with Andrews.

What did Thomas Andrews tell the captain?

430 That the ship was doomed. He calculated that it would sink within an hour and a half.

When was the first distress signal sent?

431 At about 12:10 A.M. Captain Smith handed Jack Phillips the *Titanic's* estimated position and asked him to send out a call for assistance. He immediately began tapping out the Morse-code distress call "CQD" followed by "MGY," the ship's call letters.

Why didn't he use SOS?

432 He did. "SOS" was a new international call for help. Phillips began sending it a little later at Harold Bride's suggestion. "It may be your last chance," he joked. The *Titanic* was one of the first ships in distress to send out an SOS signal.

What do CQD and SOS stand for?

433 Nothing. SOS had recently been chosen as an international distress call because it was easy to send and recognize in Morse code. (CQD does not stand for "Come Quick Distress" nor does SOS mean "Save Our Ship.")

Who replied to the distress call?

434 The *Olympic*, the *Frankfurt*, and the *Carpathia*.

Which one was the closest?

435 The *Carpathia*. When Captain Smith was told it was 58 miles (93 km) away, though, he left the wireless room without saying a word. He knew it would take hours for the *Carpathia* to reach his ship.

TO THE LIFEBOATS

How did the passengers learn about the collision?

436 Ruth Becker's mother was told by a room steward that nothing was wrong. But later she heard loud voices and poked her head out into the hallway. Another steward told Mrs. Becker to put on a life jacket and hurry to the top deck.

437 Third-class passengers Carl Jonsson and Daniel Buckley didn't have to be told to leave. Their cabins were filling with water.

Did people have time to get dressed?

438 The Beckers threw their coats on over their nightgowns. They were in such a hurry that they forgot to put on their life jackets.

439 Jack Thayer was able to put on a suit and two vests under his overcoat.

440 Frank Goldsmith's father left to find out what had happened and then told his wife to wake and dress Frank.

441 Young Douglas Spedden was dressed by his nurse and told they were taking a trip to look at the stars. His mother tucked his toy polar bear under his arm before they left.

How many life jackets did the *Titanic* carry?

442 Enough for all the passengers and crew—3,560.

A Titanic life jacket

How many lifeboats were there and how many people could get in each one?

Answers #443 – 445
● Fourteen main lifeboats (with a capacity for 65 people each).
● Two emergency sea boats (40 occupants each).
● Four collapsible boats (47 each).

What's a collapsible boat?

446 The four Engelhardt collapsible boats had wooden bottoms, but sides made of folding canvas that had to be pulled up and set in place with iron supports.

How many people in all could fit in the lifeboats?

447 Even if all 20 lifeboats had been filled to capacity, there would only have been room in them for 1,178 people. Approximately 1,029 of those on the *Titanic* during its maiden voyage were doomed.

Why weren't there enough lifeboats?

448 In 1894 the British Board of Trade set rules that required ships of 10,000 tons or more to carry at least 16 lifeboats. But these rules were not changed as ships grew rapidly in size. The *Titanic*, at over 53,000 tons (53,800 t), carried the 16 required lifeboats in addition to an extra four collapsible boats.

Where were the lifeboats kept?

449 The lifeboats were kept on the boat deck, with one row of eight down each side of the ship. The two emergency boats were swung out on davits over the edge of the ship's hull, with collapsibles C and D right beside them. Collapsibles A and B were stored on the roof of the officers' quarters.

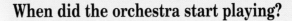

What is a davit?

450 A davit is like a tilting crane. The ropes and pulleys used to lower lifeboats are attached to it. Modern "Welin" davits had been installed on the *Titanic*, one at either end of each of the 16 main lifeboats.

When did they start loading the lifeboats?

451 The order to put women and children into lifeboats was given at 12:25 A.M.

When was the first boat lowered?

452 Lifeboat No. 7 was lowered at 12:45 A.M. with 19 aboard although it could carry 65. Movie star Dorothy Gibson and two honeymoon couples were among them.

When did the orchestra start playing?

453 The orchestra was ordered to play light and cheerful tunes to calm the passengers. They started playing at around 12:15 A.M.

Where did they play?

454 At first, the orchestra began playing in the first-class lounge on A-deck. Later, they moved up to the boat deck and played in the first-class entrance next to the Grand Staircase. Finally, they moved outside and played on deck beside the gymnasium.

Wallace Hartley (center) and his musicians played as the boats were loaded.

The first distress rocket lights up the sky.

Why wasn't it full?

455 At first most of the passengers did not believe the *Titanic* was really sinking. It seemed much nicer to stay on board a warm and bright ship, so many of the early lifeboats left half-empty. Some of the officers were also concerned that the boats might buckle if they were filled.

When were the first rockets fired?

456 At 12:55 A.M. the first white distress flare was fired into the air and burst with a loud bang. Eight rockets were fired altogether.

Why was it "women and children first"?

457 It was a traditional rule of the sea. First Officer Murdoch, who was in charge of loading the boats on the starboard side (with odd numbers), followed the rule of women and children *first*. But Second Officer Lightoller, who was in charge of the port side (boats with even numbers), was more strict, insisting on women and children *only*.

LAUNCHING *the* LIFEBOATS
12:45 to 1:30 A.M.

When were the lifeboats launched and how many people were in each one?

The information in this chart is based on eyewitness accounts. But because it was dark and no one took an official count in each lifeboat, the times and numbers below are approximate. Even by taking the witnesses' lowest estimated number of occupants for each boat, those saved amount to 815—over 100 more than actually survived.

Answers #458 – 477

Time Launched	Lifeboat No.	Total No. of Occupants (and Actual Capacity)	
12:45 A.M.	7	19	(65)
12:55 A.M.	5	41	(65)
12:55 A.M.	6	28	(65)
1:00 A.M.	3	32	(65)
1:10 A.M.	1	12	(40)
1:10 A.M.	8	28	(65)
1:20 A.M.	10	55	(65)
1:25 A.M.	14	60	(65)
1:25 A.M.	16	50	(65)
1:30 A.M.	9	56	(65)
1:30 A.M.	12	40	(65)
1:35 A.M.	11	70	(65)
1:40 A.M.	13	64	(65)
1:40 A.M.	15	70	(65)
1:45 A.M.	2	25	(40)
1:50 A.M.	4	40	(65)
2:00 A.M.	C	42	(47)
2:05 A.M.	D	40	(47)
2:20 A.M.	A*	13	(47)
2:20 A.M.	B**	30	(47)

*Floated off the deck half swamped; swimmers scrambled aboard.
**Floated off upside down; swimmers scrambled onto its back.

How far was it from the boat deck down to the water?

 478 About 60 feet (18 m), although this distance became shorter for the forward boats as the ship sank.

How much rope did it take to lower the lifeboats?

479 Six feet (2 m) of rope was required to lower each boat just 1 foot (30 cm).

Is it true some of the lifeboats nearly tipped while being lowered?

480 Since few of the crew members were experienced with lifeboats, some of the boats were lowered unevenly, causing them to tilt as one end descended much faster than the other. Passengers were terrified that they would be dumped out into the sea.

Did some boats nearly sink as soon as they reached the water?

481 All of the lifeboats had small holes in the bottom of the keel, which allowed water to drain out when they were stored on deck. As Lifeboat No. 5 was lowered, someone above shouted down, "Make sure the plug is in!" The boat had already reached the surface of the water before Quartermaster Alfred Olliver was able to plug the hole.

Were the boats just for first-class passengers?

482 The forward part of the boat deck was promenade space for first-class passengers and the rear part for second-class passengers. People from these classes thus had the best chance of getting into a lifeboat simply because they could get to them quickly and easily.

Did any passengers refuse to enter the lifeboats?

483 Ida Straus, wife of the owner of Macy's, was about to enter Lifeboat No. 8 but then refused to leave her husband. Turning to him she said, "We have been living together for many years. Where you go, I go." Both perished.

484 Alfred Rush, who had just turned 16, was offered a chance to go onto the boat deck with Frank Goldsmith and his mother. But he pulled back, saying firmly, "No. I'm staying here with the men." He died later that night.

Which boat were Douglas Spedden and his toy bear in?

485 Douglas and his bear, his mother, nurse, and mother's maid entered Lifeboat No. 3 shortly before 1:00 A.M. Because the boat was not full, Douglas's father and some other men were allowed in.

Why was it difficult for third-class passengers to reach the boat deck?

486 The cabins for third-class passengers were located deep within the bow and stern of the ship. In order for any of the steerage passengers to proceed to the lifeboats, they had to find their way through a maze of passageways. And since many of them could not read the English signs, they did not know what direction to take.

Were third-class passengers locked down below?

487 Gates had been set up throughout ships of this era to keep steerage passengers out of the first- and second-class areas. During the sinking, crew members kept the gates locked because they had not been ordered to open them. However, several stewards went below to guide third-class women and children up to the lifeboats, but some of the women refused to go without the men. By the time many of the third-class passengers reached the boat deck, the lifeboats were all gone.

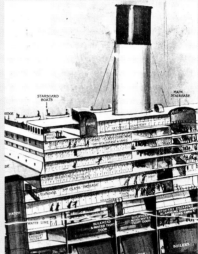

This 1912 illustration shows how difficult it was to get up to the boat deck from lower down in the ship.

Were the boats in the water supposed to pick up additional passengers?

488 Yes. It was hoped that extra passengers could climb down through the gangway doors into boats that had already been launched. During the evening, Captain Smith shouted at the boats through his megaphone, "Come alongside!" But the seamen manning the boats, fearing they would be sucked under when the ship sank, decided it would be safer to row away.

When did people realize the *Titanic* was really going to sink?

489 By 1:15 A.M. the water had reached the name *Titanic* on the bow. As the tilt of the deck grew steeper, the boats began to be more fully loaded with passengers.

"WE'RE SINKING FAST!"
1:30 to 2:00 A.M.

Did people start to panic when they realized the *Titanic* was really sinking?

490 By 1:30 A.M. some signs of panic were beginning to appear among the passengers. As portside Lifeboat No. 14 was lowered with 60 people, including Fifth Officer Lowe, a group of men on deck seemed ready to jump into the already full boat. Lowe fired three shots with his revolver to keep them away.

Did they still expect other ships to come to the rescue?

491 The lights of a steamer on the horizon seemed so close that Captain Smith had ordered Lifeboat No. 8 to row over to it, land its passengers, and come back for more. But Jack Phillips and Harold Bride in the wireless room knew that no ship in the immediate area was coming to their rescue. By 1:30 A.M. the radio calls were becoming more desperate — "We're sinking fast" and "Women and children in boats."

How did Ruth Becker manage to get into a lifeboat?

492 The Beckers had gone up to a higher deck at about 12:45, but because the night air was cold, Ruth had been sent back to their cabin for some blankets. When she returned, they went on to the boat deck and a sailor picked up Ruth's younger brother and sister and placed them in Lifeboat No. 11. When the boat began to be lowered, Mrs. Becker screamed, "Oh, please let me go with my children!" and jumped in. Seeing Ruth still on the deck, she called out, "Ruth! Get in another boat!" Ruth went to the next boat, No. 13, and the officer there picked her up and dropped her in it.

Wasn't Ruth's boat nearly crushed by another one?

493 Yes. After reaching the water, Lifeboat No. 13 drifted aft, right under descending Boat No. 15. Despite cries from the people in Ruth's boat, No. 15 kept coming down until it was so close that they could touch the bottom of it. But luckily a crewman jumped up with his knife and cut No. 13 free of its lowering ropes. Ruth's boat pushed away just as the other boat hit the water, only inches from them.

Ruth Becker with her brother

What was the last message received by the *Carpathia*?

494 At 1:45 the *Carpathia* heard its last report from the *Titanic*, "Engine room full up to boilers."

How did Billy and Lucile Carter get into a lifeboat?

495 At 1:50 the Carter children and their mother had been waiting for over an hour to enter Lifeboat No. 4. Second Officer Lightoller had ordered this boat lowered to A-deck, thinking it would be easier for passengers to board from there. But he had forgotten that the windows on A-deck had been glassed in. During the confusion, those waiting to board were ordered down from the boat deck, back up, and then down again. Eventually, the windows were opened and deck chairs were used as stairs as the boat was loaded.

Mrs. Carter

Is it true Billy was almost not allowed in?

496 While Lifeboat No. 4 was being loaded, a steward tried to prevent 13-year-old Jack Ryerson from boarding. When Jack's father insisted he go with his mother, the steward gave in but said, "No more boys." Hearing this, Billy Carter's mother put her own hat on his head, and Billy climbed into the lifeboat without any objections.

Did Mr. Carter help his family into the lifeboat?

497 No. He had left his family at Lifeboat No. 4 over an hour before, not knowing that there had been a delay in loading it. At 1:50 he was on the other side of the boat deck helping J. Bruce Ismay and the officers load third-class women and children (including Frank Goldsmith and his mother) into Collapsible Lifeboat C.

Were any other boys not allowed into boats?

498 Eleven-year-old Willie Coutts was almost refused entry into one of the last lifeboats because of his hat. His mother Minnie had enlisted the help of several crewmen to help lead her and her two boys from their third-class cabin up through a maze of stairs and passageways to the boat deck. Finally, as they went to enter a lifeboat, Willie was held back because his straw hat made him look too old. Minnie pleaded with the officer and finally Willie was allowed to escape the sinking ship.

Willie Coutts

Who else tried to get into Lifeboat No. 4?

499 John Jacob Astor asked if he could join his pregnant wife, Madeleine. Lightoller refused and Astor asked for the number of the lifeboat. As the boat was being lowered, he tossed his gloves to Madeleine. They never saw each other again.

What shocked Mrs. Ryerson in Lifeboat No. 4?

500 That it only took them a few minutes to reach the water, which was just 15 feet (5 m) below. As the boat descended down the side of the ship, she could see water swirling around the furniture in the brightly lit staterooms on B-deck.

THE LAST LIFEBOAT
2:00 to 2:17 A.M.

J. Bruce Ismay

How many people were left on board after 2:00 A.M.?

503 Over 1,500 people were clustered on the *Titanic* as her propellers began to rise out of the water.

How many boats were left?

504 Only one, Collapsible D, was left to be loaded. Collapsibles A and B were stowed on the roof of the officers' quarters.

Did J. Bruce Ismay really leave on one of the last boats?

501 Yes. As Collapsible C was being lowered at around 2:00 A.M., Ismay and then Billy Carter's father stepped into it.

Why was Collapsible C hard to lower?

502 Because the *Titanic* was leaning to port, Collapsible C's canvas sides scraped against the rivets in the *Titanic*'s starboard side. Frank Goldsmith's mother and others on board had to push the collapsible out from the hull to allow it to continue down to the water.

The ship's propellers rise out of the water (above). Crewmen link arms and an officer shoots into the air (left) to prevent a rush on the last boats.

How did the crew prevent a rush on Collapsible D?

505 Second Officer Lightoller had the crew form a ring around the boat. Only women and children were allowed through the locked arms of the men.

Was anyone shot?

506 The officers fired shots into the air to control the crowds, but it is not known if anyone was actually shot.

Is it true two baby boys were handed through the crewmen's ring?

507 Yes. Mr. Navratil, who was using the name "Hoffman" because he had kidnapped his two sons from his wife, put them into the last lifeboat.

Did any men jump into the last lifeboat?

508 Yes. Hugh Woolner and Håkan Björnström-Steffanson jumped into Collapsible D from A-deck.

Did they keep on sending SOS messages?

509 At around 2:05, Captain Smith entered the wireless room and released Phillips and Bride from their duties, telling them, "You can do no more. Now it's every man for himself." But Phillips went right on working and a faint distress message was heard by a ship called the *Virginian* as late as 2:17 A.M.

Did the orchestra play until the end?

510 It is believed that the band played until after 2:00 A.M. Due to the increasing tilt of the deck, it is unlikely they would have been able to play right to the end.

Did they really play "Nearer My God to Thee"?

511 Some survivors said that they did. Harold Bride, though, claimed that the last song played was "Autumn." He may have been referring to a popular waltz tune of the day.

What happened once people realized there were no more boats?

Answers #512 – 521

● The hundreds of people left behind stood quietly on the upper decks.

● Jack Thayer and his new friend Milton Long exchanged messages for each other's families, and Jack thought about the future pleasures he probably would not enjoy.

● Two-year-old Loraine Allison grasped her parents' hands. Nurse Alice Cleaver had taken her baby brother into a lifeboat, but her parents had waited until it was too late.

Jack Thayer

● Groups of men struggled to free Collapsibles A and B from the roof of the officers' quarters.

● Some people jumped overboard. Others threw deck chairs, doors, and casks overboard to use as rafts.

● Father Thomas Byles recited the rosary, heard confessions, and gave absolutions to more than 100 passengers.

● Tennis player R. Norris Williams and his father, Charles D., felt it was too cold to remain out on deck, so they went into the gym to ride the exercise bicycles.

R. Norris Williams

● Archibald Butt, Arthur Ryerson, Francis D. Millet, and Clarence Moore made their way to the first-class smoking room to play one last hand of cards.

● Journalist William T. Stead, who had written articles predicting a great maritime

Archibald W. Butt

disaster if ships went to sea without enough lifeboats, also went to the smoking room, where he sat down in a leather chair to read a book.

● The ship's builder, Thomas Andrews, was also last seen in the smoking room, staring into space, his life jacket cast aside.

"EVERY MAN *for* HIMSELF!"

What happened when the bow of the *Titanic* began to plunge into the ocean?

522 A giant wave swept up the deck, washing many people into the sea. At the same time, the guy wires supporting the forward funnel snapped; the funnel fell over with a cloud of soot and sparks, crushing dozens of swimmers in the water, including John Jacob Astor and R. Norris Williams' father, Charles. Shortly after the funnel collapsed, water began crashing through the dome over the Grand Staircase.

What did Milton Long and Jack Thayer do?

523 Jack Thayer had wanted to slide down a rope and swim to a lifeboat, but Milton Long was not a very good swimmer and had begged his friend to stay. When the wave began surging toward them, they had no choice but to swim for it. Jack jumped out as far as he could, and later made it to Collapsible B. Sadly, Milton chose to slide down the ship's hull. Jack never saw him again.

How long did Jack Phillips and Harold Bride stay in the wireless room?

524 After Captain Smith had released them from duty, Phillips continued to call desperately for help. Bride went into their personal quarters to gather his spare money. When he returned he found a stoker trying to steal Phillips' life jacket. Bride held the man while Phillips punched him and they left him lying on the floor. As they ran out on deck, they could hear the sound of water washing over the bridge.

As the hull plunges downward (above left), water crashes through the wrought-iron and glass dome over the Grand Staircase (above right).

How long did the lights stay on?

525 The lights stayed on until two minutes before the *Titanic* sank. The engineers working down in the bowels of the ship had kept the power going, with no hope of saving themselves. Then the lights went out forever and the ship began to tear apart.

What happened to Collapsibles A and B?

526 Those struggling to launch them tried using oars as a ramp, hoping the collapsibles could be slid down onto the boat deck. But they were both so heavy, the collapsibles smashed the oars. Collapsible A landed upright, and men began attaching it to the davits, while B rolled over and landed upside down. When water surged up the boat deck, Collapsible A broke loose and floated off. Because its canvas sides had not yet been raised, it was half-flooded. Collapsible B, meanwhile, was carried overboard, still upside down.

What happened to the dogs on board?

527 A passenger went to the kennels and released them after the lifeboats had all gone. Survivor R. Norris Williams later found himself face to face in the water with the champion bulldog, Gamon de Pycombe.

THE FINAL MOMENTS

Did the ship really break in two?

528 Until the *Titanic* was discovered in 1985, most people believed that it had sunk in one piece. Several witnesses claimed the ship broke up (Jack Thayer even had a series of sketches drawn showing this). But the highest ranking officer to survive, Charles Lightoller, insisted it had not. Because of his testimony, the British Board of Trade inquiry declared that the *Titanic* "sank intact."

How did it break in half?

529 The stress on the steel hull was so great that it could not support the weight of the stern as it rose out of the water. Since the stern section contained the heavy engines and turbine, the *Titanic* began to break apart between the third and fourth funnels.

After he was rescued, Jack Thayer described the **Titanic's** *sinking to* **Carpathia** *passenger L.D. Skidmore, who drew the rough sketches below.*

Was there a suction whirlpool?

531 No. The stern section sank so slowly that Chief Baker Charles Joughin stepped off into the water without even getting his hair wet. Unfortunately, the seamen manning the lifeboats had feared that there would be a suction whirlpool, and as a result they rowed as far away as they could from the ship.

What happened to Captain Smith?

532 It is not clear what happened to Captain Smith. One survivor said he jumped into the sea as the wave rushed up the deck. Two survivors claimed to have seen him swimming in the water, encouraging the men scrambling aboard Collapsible B. Less reliable reports claim he called out, "Be British!" before going down with his ship.

What time did the *Titanic* disappear beneath the surface?

536 In Lifeboat No. 5, Third Officer Pitman announced that it was 2:20 A.M.

How did Harold Bride survive?

533 Harold Bride had been trying to help with Collapsible B when it was washed overboard. Holding onto an oarlock, Harold was carried off the ship with the lifeboat. He then found himself in the water beneath the overturned boat, but soon swam out and climbed atop its keel. Phillips had gone toward the stern after the two men left the wireless room. He did not survive.

What happened to the stern section?

530 The stern section fell back until it was almost level again, although it was still attached to the bow along the bottom of the keel like a giant hinge. However, as gravity pulled the bow (which was completely full of water) toward the seabed, the stern section was drawn upright once more before the two halves finally separated. Then the stern silently bobbed in the water for a minute or so before it, too, slowly began to sink.

How did Jack Thayer survive?

534 After he hit the water, Jack was sucked down. When he surfaced the ship was about 40 feet (12 m) away from him. His hand grabbed what turned out to be overturned Collapsible B and, like Harold Bride, he pulled himself up onto it. The overturned boat provided a refuge for 30 men, including Archibald Gracie and Second Officer Lightoller.

What happened to Collapsible A?

535 Although it was half-submerged, over a dozen people climbed into it, including R. Norris Williams and third-class passenger Rosa Abbott, the only woman to struggle on board.

"IT'S GONE"

How did the people in the lifeboats react when the *Titanic* disappeared?

537 Ada Clarke in Lifeboat No. 14 (with Eva Hart and her mother) heard somebody say, "It's gone," but she was so cold she didn't pay much attention.

538 Douglas Spedden slept in his nurse's lap.

539 Frank Goldsmith's mother pressed his head against her chest so he could not hear the sound of wailing voices.

540 To Jack Thayer clinging to overturned Collapsible B, the sound was "a long continuous wailing chant."

How cold was the water?

541 At the time the *Titanic* foundered, the temperature of the water was only 28°F (-2°C). Most of those struggling in the water in their life jackets would have succumbed to hypothermia, while others may have had heart attacks.

Who survived the longest swimming in the water?

542 During the sinking, Chief Baker Charles Joughin twice went down to his cabin in order to drink a glass of whiskey. After riding the stern down (he later said it felt like riding in an elevator), Joughin paddled around in the water. He barely noticed the cold because of the alcohol he had drunk. Unable to climb aboard Collapsible B, he held on to the hand of his friend John Maynard. At daybreak, the chief baker was pulled aboard Boat No. 12. Altogether, Joughin had been in the water for two hours!

Why didn't the lifeboats go back to rescue people?

543 Although several passengers and crew members wanted to go back, the majority protested out of fear that the hundreds in the water would swamp the boats. As Quartermaster Robert Hichens selfishly snapped in Boat No. 6, "It is our lives now, not theirs."

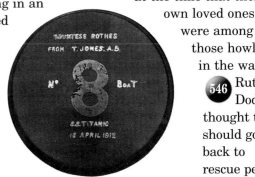

A plaque with Lifeboat No. 8's number on it

Didn't the women in the lifeboats realize it was their husbands and sons that were drowning?

545 Most of the women in the boats did not seem to realize at the time that their own loved ones were among those howling in the water.

546 Ruth Dodge thought they should go back to rescue people in the water, but the others in Lifeboat No. 5 disagreed. She was so upset with them that she later switched to Boat No. 7.

547 In Lifeboat No. 8 the Countess of Rothes, her cousin Gladys Cherry, Seaman Thomas Jones, and one American woman wanted to return but the rest of the people in the boat overruled them. "Ladies," said Jones, "if any of us are saved, remember I wanted to go back. I would rather drown with them than leave them."

What are the symptoms of hypothermia?

544 The first symptom of hypothermia is shivering, which gradually lessens as the body's temperature drops. Victims' pulses become slow and weak, and their breathing becomes shallow. Then they grow very sleepy and confused, and may suffer from hallucinations before finally losing consciousness.

The role played by women survivors in the lifeboats is captured in this 1912 magazine illustration.
In Lifeboat No. 8, Seaman Jones handed over the tiller to the Countess of Rothes and later gave her a plaque
(opposite) in gratitude for her assistance that night.

Which lifeboat did return?

548 After the sinking, Lifeboat No. 4 was still fairly close by. Under the direction of Quartermaster Walter Perkis, they picked up five men, two of whom later died. After Boat No. 4 tied up with boats 10, 12, 14, and D, Fifth Officer Lowe redistributed the occupants of No. 14 and headed back into the mass of floundering people. Lowe was only able to rescue four, one of whom later died.

Fifth Officer Lowe

How long did the people in the water last?

549 After about 20 minutes, the wailing gradually began to die away until by 3:00 A.M. all was quiet.

Did anyone survive by clinging to wreckage?

550 No. The only swimmers who survived (apart from Baker Joughin) were either pulled into lifeboats or climbed into swamped Collapsible A or onto the back of overturned Collapsible B.

Couldn't people have clambered up onto floating icebergs?

551 There were no icebergs near enough to the site of the sinking.

Why didn't the people in swamped Collapsible A bail out the water?

552 They tried. One man wanted to borrow another's hat for bailing but the owner refused, saying he would catch cold—even though he was already soaked. After struggling to raise Boat A's collapsible canvas sides, they discovered the supports were broken. Then they prayed as a group standing in the freezing water.

Did other people pray?

553 The 30 men clinging to overturned Collapsible B recited the Lord's Prayer.

THE LONG NIGHT

Was there anything to eat or drink in the lifeboats?

554 While the boats had been equipped with a water beaker and provision tank, and tins of biscuits had been placed into each, it seems that in most cases they were never discovered by those on board.

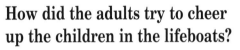

This hardtack biscuit (left) was saved from the supplies packed in one of the lifeboats.

How did the adults try to cheer up the children in the lifeboats?

555 Some parents put on a brave face and made jokes in an effort to comfort their children.

556 Bessie Watt told her daughter Bertha to pretend they were rowing on Loch Ness.

557 Edith Rosenbaum entertained a baby with her lucky toy pig that played a tune whenever its tail was wound.

558 Others fed cookies to the children or pointed out the stars. It was a very clear night and the constellations and Milky Way were easily spotted. One woman was fascinated by all the shooting stars she could see.

How did people try to stay warm?

559 Most people in the lifeboats had dressed warmly, and those who had not, wrapped themselves in blankets offered by other passengers. Ruth Becker gave the blankets her mother had sent her to get from their cabin to the crew members in Boat No. 13 who were dressed in only thin clothing. She also gave another man a handkerchief to wrap around his injured finger, and promised to help a woman find her baby (who had been placed into Boat No. 11).

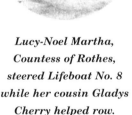

Lucy-Noel Martha, Countess of Rothes, steered Lifeboat No. 8 while her cousin Gladys Cherry helped row.

Is it true a baby was nearly thrown overboard?

560 Yes. The infant belonging to the woman Ruth Becker had promised to help was mistaken for a bundle of clothing. In order to create more space in the overcrowded boat, the baby was nearly thrown overboard, but its cry saved its life just in time.

Did any of the dogs survive?

561 Yes. Margaret Hays' Pomeranian was taken into a lifeboat as was Elizabeth Rothschild's dog and Henry Sleeper Harper's brown Pekinese, which was called Sun Yat Sen.

Who rowed the lifeboats?

562 Most of the crew members who were ordered into the boats had no experience in handling them. As a result, many passengers helped row the lifeboats; this also helped keep them warm.

How were the lifeboats steered?

563 Each lifeboat was equipped with a "tiller," a bar used to turn the rudder to port or starboard. In Boat No. 8, the Countess of Rothes handled the tiller most of the night.

Were there any lights in the lifeboats?

564 Like the food and water provisions which were supposed to be in each boat, the lights aboard were not found by passengers and crewmen in most of the boats.

How did the survivors in the lifeboats signal for help or to other lifeboats?

565 Fourth Officer Boxhall lit flares, Frank Goldsmith's mother set her straw hat on fire and raised it on an oar, and Ella White waved her cane with its built-in electric light. Unfortunately, people in other boats often mistook these for the lights of ships.

When did the lifeboats first see the rescue ship?

566 The first rockets from the *Carpathia* were sighted at about 3:30 A.M.

What did the survivors see when the sun started to rise?

567 An enormous field of ice, in every shape and size, stretched off to the north. Icebergs as much as 200 feet (60 m) high sparkled in shades of white, pink, blue, and purple. Douglas Spedden in Lifeboat No. 3 woke up and said, "Look at the beautiful North Pole with no Santa Claus on it."

How long were people in the lifeboats before they were rescued?

568 From the time of the sinking until they were rescued, the survivors were in the lifeboats between two and six hours.

How did Molly Brown earn the nickname "Unsinkable?"

569 Molly Brown was in Lifeboat No. 6. Quartermaster Hichens (who had been at the wheel of the *Titanic* when it struck the iceberg) was in charge, but his behavior infuriated everyone in the

lifeboat, particularly Molly. He refused to go back to rescue people, saying they would only find "stiffs." He also yelled at the two men who were rowing, and muttered predictions that they would be left drifting for days. Molly Brown suggested that he hand over the tiller to a woman and help the other men row. Hichens rudely refused. Molly picked up an oar, began rowing, and encouraged other women to do the same. Later, when the *Carpathia* was sighted in the early morning light, Hichens insisted it had not come to rescue them but was there only to pick up dead bodies. At this Molly Brown lost all patience. She threatened to throw Hichens overboard if he interfered and ordered those rowing to head for the *Carpathia*. Her actions would later be celebrated (and exaggerated) in books, movies, and a musical called *The Unsinkable Molly Brown*.

THE CARPATHIA *to the* RESCUE

What kind of ship was the *Carpathia*?

570 The Cunard ship *Carpathia* could carry 2,550 passengers but on this voyage had only 743. They had boarded in New York on April 11, 1912, for a Mediterranean cruise.

Who was the *Carpathia's* captain?

571 Arthur Henry Rostron, aged 43, was nicknamed the "Electric Spark" in recognition of his energy, eagerness, and quick decision-making.

Captain Rostron (inset) was later awarded for his role in the rescue (above).

What orders did Captain Rostron give to prepare his ship for the rescue?

Answers #572 – 581

● One doctor would turn each of the three dining rooms into a makeshift hospital.
● A steward in each corridor would keep those on board out of the way.
● Hot drinks and soup were prepared.
● Blankets were collected.
● All spare berths were to be utilized for the *Titanic's* passengers, along with the smoking rooms, library, and officers' cabins.
● Oil was readied to dump overboard to calm heaving ocean swells.
● Lifeboats were swung out.
● Gangway doors were opened.
● Ropes, chair slings, and ladders were hung.
● The purser, assistants, and stewards would direct the survivors and take names.

Why was it dangerous for the *Carpathia* to go to the *Titanic's* rescue?

582 Captain Rostron knew that a large field of ice lay ahead in the dark, and he posted several extra lookouts to watch for the dangerous bergs.

How many icebergs did they have to steer around?

583 Six.

What was the *Carpathia's* top speed?

584 Its normal speed was 14.5 knots, but Rostron ordered machinery and heating systems shut down to gain extra steam for the engines. On this night, the *Carpathia* went almost 17.5 knots!

How did they signal the *Titanic* survivors?

585 Captain Rostron ordered rockets to be fired every 15 minutes, beginning at 2:45 A.M. At 3:30 they arrived near the *Titanic's* sinking position.

What guided the *Carpathia* to the *Titanic's* survivors?

586 When the passengers first saw the *Carpathia's* signals at 3:30 in the morning, they burned newspapers, personal letters, and handkerchiefs. Fourth Officer Boxhall in Lifeboat No. 2 also fired the last of his green flares.

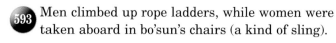

Why were the men on Collapsible B afraid that they wouldn't be rescued in time?

587 As morning dawned, the wind picked up and the overturned boat rocked in the swell. This caused the air beneath to leak out even faster.

Who rescued them?

588 Those on Collapsible B were rescued in the nick of time by boats No. 12 and 4.

What did those in Collapsible A do to try and attract the *Carpathia*'s attention?

589 They counted to three and screamed over and over.

Who rescued them?

590 Boat No. 14 passed by and took them aboard.

Which lifeboat reached the *Carpathia* first?

591 Boat No. 2 came alongside the *Carpathia* at 4:10 A.M.

Who was the first survivor to board the *Carpathia*?

592 Elisabeth Allen, a 22-year-old heiress from St. Louis.

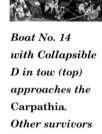

Boat No. 14 with Collapsible D in tow (top) approaches the Carpathia. Other survivors (above and right) wait to be taken on board.

How did the adults get on board?

593 Men climbed up rope ladders, while women were taken aboard in bo'sun's chairs (a kind of sling).

How were the children pulled on board?

594 They were hoisted up in canvas ashbags.

Why was No. 12 the last lifeboat to reach the *Carpathia*?

595 Boat No. 12 had taken on extra passengers from Boat No. 14 as well as some of the men from Collapsible B. With at least 75 people in it, the boat was so crowded that its sides were only inches above the waves. It finally rowed up to the *Carpathia* at 8:30 A.M.

Who was the last survivor to board the *Carpathia*?

596 Second Officer Charles Lightoller, the highest-ranking surviving officer, was the last survivor to climb aboard.

Did the *Carpathia* find any survivors in the water?

597 No. Only those in the boats were rescued. By this time, most of the wreckage had drifted away, and the *Carpathia* passed only one body.

How long did the rescue operation take?

598 Over four hours.

How many people were rescued?

599 Seven hundred five.

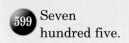

What was Ruth Becker's saddest memory of the tragedy?

600 With the survivors aboard, the *Carpathia* started its engines and headed for New York. But the rails were still lined with women waiting for their husbands, fathers, and sons. Ruth remembered seeing these women being led away in tears, finally realizing that their loved ones had died.

THE MYSTERY SHIP

Did another ship show up at the rescue scene?

601 Yes. At 8:30 A.M. on April 15, 1912, the *Californian* arrived near the *Carpathia*.

Was this the nearby ship that didn't come to the *Titanic's* rescue?

602 Many of the *Titanic*'s passengers and crew members clearly saw the lights of a ship off in the distance. Officers even tried to signal it with their Morse lamp. But the mysterious ship never came to help. Both the American and British inquiries into the disaster concluded that the ship in question was the *Californian*. But some people feel that the *Californian* and its captain, Stanley Lord, have been unfairly blamed.

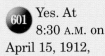

Was Captain Stanley Lord (top) of the Californian *(above) guilty of not coming to the* Titanic's *aid?*

What was the *Californian* doing in the area the night of the sinking?

603 The *Californian* was a cargo vessel that had left London on April 5, and was sailing to Boston, Massachusetts. On Sunday, April 14, Captain Lord saw an enormous field of ice lying ahead of his path, and decided to sit out the night. He ordered the engines stopped at 10:21 P.M.

Did the *Californian* warn the *Titanic* about the ice?

604 Cyril Evans, the *Californian*'s wireless operator, notified the *Titanic* at around 10:55 P.M. that they were stopped and surrounded by ice (see p. 41) but Jack Phillips, who was behind in his work, angrily told him, "Keep out! Shut up!"

Did any of the *Californian's* crew see another ship in the area?

605 Captain Lord himself noticed a steamer approaching from the southeast just before 11:00 P.M., and asked Cyril Evans what other ships were nearby. Evans told him that the *Titanic* was fairly close, but Lord felt that the ship he had seen was too small to be the *Titanic*.

Did they try to signal it?

606 Between 12:10 and 1:50 A.M. two of the *Californian*'s officers and one crewman each tried to signal the distant ship with a flashing Morse lamp. Although this lamp could shine a distance of 10 miles (16 km), they received no response.

Did they see any rockets?

607 Yes. At 12:45 A.M., the *Californian*'s second officer saw a flash of light he at first believed to be a shooting star. But when a second one exploded in the sky, he realized they were rockets. Those on board the *Californian* counted eight rockets altogether, the same number as fired by the *Titanic*.

Do white rockets at sea always indicate a ship in distress?

608 Yes.

Why didn't the *Californian* hear the *Titanic*'s SOS messages?

609 After being so rudely cut off by Jack Phillips, Cyril Evans immediately stopped tapping out messages and at 11:30 P.M., he went to bed.

How long did the *Californian*'s crew watch the other ship?

610 The second officer and a crewman continued to watch the ship on the horizon until they could no longer see its lights. Around the same time that the *Titanic* sank, those on the *Californian* thought the ship in view had steamed away.

Some of the Californian's *crew at the British inquiry*

How far away was the *Californian* from the *Titanic*?

611 Captain Lord claimed that his ship was stopped 19 ½ miles (31 km) from the *Titanic*'s reported distress position. At this distance, they would not have been able to see each other due to the curvature of the Earth. Yet people on both the *Titanic* and the *Californian* believed that the ship they could see was only about 5 miles (8 km) away.

Were there any other boats nearby?

612 Sailing records from 1912 indicate that there were up to ten ships in the area where the *Titanic* went down, and several could be seen by the *Carpathia* the morning after the sinking.

Could there have been a third ship between the *Titanic* and the *Californian*?

613 Possibly. There have been many theories about this.

When did the *Californian* hear that the *Titanic* had sunk?

614 The ship's chief officer woke up Cyril Evans around 5:30 in the morning and asked him to inquire about the ship firing rockets in the night. It was then that they learned the shocking news and headed for the site of the disaster. As the *Carpathia* departed with the survivors, the *Californian* agreed to search for any others. They found no one alive.

Could the *Californian* have saved everyone on board the *Titanic*?

615 Probably not. It took the *Californian* two hours to reach the *Carpathia* in daylight. Had it proceeded to the scene immediately after the launch of the first rocket, it would have taken even longer to steer through the ice field in the dark. By then, those in the water would already have frozen to death.

THE VOYAGE *to* NEW YORK

What did Billy Carter's father do once he was on board the *Carpathia*?

616 Mr. Carter stood at the railing watching the other boats come in. When Lifeboat No. 4 came alongside, he caught sight of his wife and daughter but could not see his son. Leaning out over the rail, he called out, "Where's my son?" Still wearing his mother's hat, Billy lifted the brim and called out, "Here I am, Father, here I am!" The Carters were given a small private cabin.

Survivors on the deck of the Carpathia

What happened to Frank Goldsmith and his mother after they arrived on the *Carpathia*?

617 Frank's mother was asked her name and class by a purser and then they were given hot drinks and blankets. They waited for Frank's father to arrive, but he was not among the survivors. The Goldsmiths were given straw mattresses in the second-class dining saloon along with other third-class women and children.

What upset the Speddens?

618 Douglas Spedden's parents worked hard to help those who were suffering. His mother wrote to a friend, "We spend our time sitting on people who are cruel enough to say that no steerage should have been saved, as if they weren't human beings!"

What did Frank's mother do to pass the time?

619 She sewed emergency clothes from blankets (above) for those who had escaped wearing only pajamas or nightgowns.

Did Ruth Becker find her family?

620 While she was helping thes mother from her lifeboat search for her baby, a woman came and told Ruth that her own mother was looking everywhere for her. A few moments later she was reunited with her mother, sister, and brother. Later Ruth discovered that her friend from the lifeboat had found her child.

What were the last things taken on board the *Carpathia*?

621 Thirteen of the *Titanic*'s lifeboats. The rest were set adrift. (Collapsible A had already been set adrift during the night with three bodies in it after 13 people had been rescued from it by another lifeboat.)

What happened as the *Carpathia* passed the spot where the *Titanic* sank?

622 A memorial service was conducted in memory of those who had died in the disaster.

Who stayed in Captain Rostron's own quarters?

623 First-class passengers Madeleine Astor, Eleanor Widener, and Marian Thayer. All three were now widows.

Where did J. Bruce Ismay stay?

624 Close to shock, Ismay kept to himself in the cabin of one of the *Carpathia*'s doctors. At the suggestion of Captain Rostron, he sent notification of the disaster to White Star's New York office.

Is it true that a survivor's baby was kidnapped on board the *Carpathia*?

625 Yes. Two-year-old Phyllis Quick was snatched by a woman who could not find her own child. Phyllis was eventually returned to her mother.

Is it true the *Carpathia*'s doctors wanted to amputate someone's legs?

626 Yes. R. Norris Williams' legs had been badly frozen from standing all night in the swamped Collapsible A. But Williams insisted he could recuperate by getting up to walk every two hours, day or night. He gradually recovered, and his legs were saved. He later won several tennis championships in the United States.

Why couldn't anybody contact the *Carpathia* for news of the disaster?

627 Captain Rostron thought it was more important to transmit the names of those saved and lost, in addition to private messages.

Who helped send wireless messages from the *Carpathia*?

628 Although he was suffering from frostbite and damaged feet from his night on Collapsible B, Harold Bride agreed to help out the *Carpathia*'s wireless operator with the huge number of messages that had to be sent.

What were some of those messages?

Answers #629 – 632

● *"Deeply regret advise you* Titanic *sank this morning after collision with iceberg, resulting in serious loss of life. Full particulars later."* (Bruce Ismay)

J. Bruce Ismay sent this telegram to White Star's New York office.

● *"Jack Margaret and I safe no news yet of Mr. Thayer. Sam and Gamble meet me."* (Marian Thayer)

● *"All safe. Notify family & friends."* (Douglas Spedden's father)

● *"The ship sank B M & I are safe."* (Irish emigrant Eugene Daly)

What alarmed the survivors the second night on the *Carpathia*?

633 A storm began on Tuesday night and continued during the entire voyage to New York. Some even mistook the thunder for yet another collision with an iceberg.

How long did it take to get to New York?

634 After picking up the *Titanic* survivors on Monday morning, the *Carpathia* took three and a half days to reach New York. It steamed into the harbor on the evening of Thursday, April 18.

THE WORLD REACTS

What did the first newspaper headlines say about the disaster?

Answers #635 – 637

● "ALL SAVED FROM *TITANIC* AFTER COLLISION . . . LINER IS BEING TOWED TO HALIFAX" (*New York Evening Sun*, April 15, 1912)

● "PASSENGERS SAFELY MOVED AND STEAMER *TITANIC* TAKEN IN TOW" (*Christian Science Monitor*, April 15, 1912)

● "*TITANIC* SUNK, NO LIVES LOST" (*Daily Mail*, London, England, April 16, 1912)

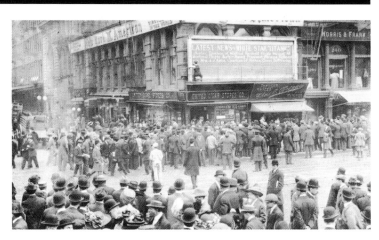

Crowds gather outside the office of a New York newspaper to find out the latest news about the disaster.

Why were they so wrong?

638 News of the *Titanic*'s sinking had been sent from ship to ship by wireless, but the first reports contained little accurate information. It wasn't until 6:20 P.M. on April 15 that the White Star offices learned the truth in a telegram from the *Olympic*.

When was the first public list of survivors posted?

639 It was handwritten on a large board outside the offices of the *New York Times* in the early hours of April 16.

Who was the first reporter to interview survivors?

640 Carlos F. Hurd, a reporter for the *St. Louis Post-Dispatch* and the *New York World*, was a passenger on board the *Carpathia*. In addition to interviewing many of the *Titanic*'s survivors, he and his wife took care of two-year-old Edmond Navratil, who stayed with them in their cabin.

What did Ruth Becker see as the *Carpathia* entered New York harbor on April 18?

641 Dozens of yachts, tugs, and other boats surrounded the ship. Many had been hired by reporters, who shouted questions to the *Carpathia*'s crew and passengers through megaphones.

How did Carlos Hurd deliver his story to the *New York World*?

642 The *World* hired a tugboat and Hurd tossed a parcel containing the story to a fellow worker in the tug. The story appeared in newspapers the next day.

What did the *Carpathia* do before docking?

643 It stopped opposite the White Star pier to deposit the *Titanic*'s lifeboats. They were lowered into the harbor and each one was rowed to the pier by two *Titanic* crew members. It was the last job they would do as members of the *Titanic*'s crew.

How large was the crowd waiting for the ship?

644 At 8:00 P.M., 30,000 people crowded around Cunard's Pier 54 while another 10,000 filled the streets leading up to the docks.

Who were the first to leave the *Carpathia*?

645 At 9:00 P.M. the *Titanic* passengers from first class began filing down the gangway. Among them was Madeleine Astor, who was met by her stepson and quickly helped into a waiting car, along with her nurse and maid.

Who had to be carried off the ship?

646 Harold Bride (above). His feet were still bandaged from his ordeal on Collapsible B.

Who gave a false name to reporters?

647 Alice Cleaver (see p. 34) carried baby Trevor Allison, the only survivor from his family, off the *Carpathia*. Perhaps afraid of revealing her background, she gave her name as "Jane."

What was it like for Ruth Becker as she walked down the *Carpathia*'s gangway?

648 Ruth wore an old cloak and a blanket for a skirt, not enough to keep her warm on the cold, rainy night. It was difficult for the Beckers to see the friends who were meeting them through the crowds and the flashes from the photographers' magnesium flares. Finally they did, and were led out to a waiting car.

Did some of the people waiting at the pier not know that their loved ones had died?

649 Yes. For every joyous reunion there was one that would never take place. One man who learned that all his family members had died became hysterical. By midnight a small group remaining on the pier realized their wait was hopeless and left in tears.

What happened to Frank Goldsmith and his mother?

650 They were looked after by the Salvation Army and given new clothes and train tickets to Detroit where Mrs. Goldsmith's sister lived.

The Carpathia *lowers the* Titanic's *lifeboats in New York.*

What happened to the Navratil brothers?

651 Margaret Hays of New York, who spoke French, offered to take care of the *Titanic* orphans until their family could be found. Newspapers around the world carried the sad story of the two "orphans of the *Titanic*." In France, their mother immediately recognized the boys in a newspaper report and contacted White Star. The company quickly arranged her passage across the Atlantic and she was reunited with her sons on May 16.

Who was waiting to greet J. Bruce Ismay?

652 Two U.S. senators with a summons for him to appear the next day before a Senate inquiry into the disaster.

"THE LOVE *of* OUR HEARTS"

How did they recover the bodies of the *Titanic's* victims?

653 The White Star Line chartered the small steamer *Mackay-Bennett*, which left Halifax on April 17 to search the scene of the disaster.

Victims of the disaster lie on the Mackay-Bennett's foredeck.

How many bodies did it find?

654 Three hundred six. Most of the victims were found floating, kept upright by their life preservers, and looked as though they were sleeping. Their watches were stopped between 2:00 and 2:20 A.M.

Crew members recover a body.

Did the *Mackay-Bennett's* crew bury any bodies at sea?

655 Yes. Of the 306 bodies, 116 were too seriously injured or decomposed to be identified and were buried at sea.

How were the remaining bodies identified?

656 By information in wallets, photographs, and other items in their pockets. Initials sewn on clothing or handkerchiefs also helped.

Could they identify everyone this way?

657 No. One man had six diamonds sewn into the lining of his coat, but carried no clue to his identity. He and others like him would have to be identified by relatives once the ship returned to Halifax.

Horse-drawn hearses take bodies to a temporary morgue in Halifax.

How was John Jacob Astor identified?

658 His body was found crushed and covered with soot, which would suggest that he was killed when the forward funnel toppled over. His body was identified by the initials inside his collar, some jewelry, and by a pocketbook containing £225 and $2,440 in cash.

How long was the search?

659 Nine days.

Where were the bodies kept on board the ship?

660 The victims were prepared for burial by a team of embalmers. The first-class passengers were then placed in coffins and stored on deck. The second- and third-class passengers were sewn into canvas bags and put in the ice-filled hold.

How did the people of Halifax honor the dead as the *Mackay-Bennett* returned to port on April 30?

661 Flags flew at half staff and church bells tolled.

Were any other ships sent out?

662 The steamer *Minia* relieved the *Mackay-Bennett*. After a week, it had recovered 17 bodies. Bad weather had by now scattered the victims as far as 130 miles (209 km) from the scene of the sinking. The *Montmagny* and the *Algerine* followed the *Minia*, but after only five more bodies were found, the search was abandoned.

Were any other bodies found later?

663 First-Class Saloon Steward W.F. Cheverton was found by the steamer *Ilford* in June and was buried at sea. Other bodies seen by passing steamers were never recovered.

What else was recovered from the area of the disaster?

Answers #664 – 666
● An elaborately carved piece of oak paneling from above the forward entrance in the first-class lounge (similar to the one Rose floated on in the movie *Titanic*, although smaller).
● A deck chair.
● A piece of an oak newel post from one of the first-class staircases.

What served as a temporary morgue in Halifax?

667 The bodies were taken from the dockyard to the Mayflower Curling Rink, where relatives waited to identify the victims.

Was every body identified?

668 No. Photographs were taken of unidentified bodies before they were buried in the hope that future identification might be made. A small blond-haired boy who could not be identified became known as the "unknown child." (Researchers now believe that he may have been two-year-old Gosta Leonard Paulsson, the youngest child of third-class passenger Alma Paulsson.)

How many bodies were recovered in all?

669 Three hundred twenty-eight were retrieved by the four ships.

Where are the victims buried?

670 Fifty-nine victims were claimed by relatives and buried elsewhere. The remaining 150 were buried in three Halifax cemeteries: the Baron de Hirsch Jewish Cemetery, the Protestant Fairview Cemetery, and the Catholic Mount Olivet Cemetery. The *Mackay-Bennett*'s crew provided a funeral service and a grave marker at Fairview for the "unknown child."

Herbert Jupe

What happened to the jewelry and wallets found on the bodies?

671 Personal belongings were given to relatives in Halifax. Items not claimed there were sent to the provincial secretary's office, which then wrote to the families of the victims. The father of crewman Herbert Jupe replied with a touching letter from Belfast:
"...We are extremely obliged for all your kindness to my Precious Boy... He was not Married and was the Love of our Hearts... Please send along the Watch and Handkerchief marked H.J."

Were any members of the orchestra found?

672 Yes. Orchestra leader Wallace Hartley's body was found and returned to his hometown in England for burial. Violinist Jock Hume and bass player Fred Clark are both buried in Halifax.

What did violinist Jock Hume's family receive from his employers after the disaster?

673 The Black Talent Agency sent them a bill for $3.50 to cover the cost of his unpaid uniform.

ASKING QUESTIONS

Was there an investigation into the tragedy?

674 The day after the *Carpathia* landed, a committee of the United States Senate began holding hearings. They ran from Friday, April 19, to Saturday, May 25, 1912.

Who conducted the inquiry?

675 Senator William Alden Smith of Michigan proposed the investigation and was its chief examiner.

What questions did the American Senate inquiry want answered?

Answers #676 – 679
● Did the *Titanic* have enough lifesaving devices and had they been adequately inspected?
● Was the ship's route a dangerous one?
● Was the *Titanic* going too fast?
● Did the crew behave properly?

Who was the first witness at the inquiry?

680 J. Bruce Ismay.

Was he blamed for the tragedy?

681 Many people thought that J. Bruce Ismay should have gone down with the ship. But Ismay insisted he had only stepped into Collapsible C because no more women were in sight. He was also accused of persuading Captain Smith to make the *Titanic* go faster. The Senate inquiry was unable to find any proof of this but concluded that Ismay's presence alone may have encouraged the *Titanic's* captain to increase the ship's speed.

Who were the other star witnesses?

682 Second Officer Charles Lightoller defended the actions of Captain Smith, and wireless operator Harold Bride recounted the frantic efforts of Jack Phillips to call other ships for help.

Did the Senate inquiry question the captain and crew of the *Californian*?

683 Yes. It concluded that the *Californian* was less than 19 miles (31 km) away and could have come to the rescue in time.

What recommendations did the Senate inquiry make?

Answers #685 – 689
● Ships should carry enough lifeboats for everyone on board.
● Regular lifeboat drills should be conducted.
● Crew members should be skilled in lowering and rowing lifeboats.
● Ships should be equipped with at least two searchlights.
● Wireless on ships should be in operation 24 hours a day.

How many witnesses were questioned?

684 Eighty-two.

A newspaper cartoon from 1912 shows people gossiping about J. Bruce Ismay.

What else did Senator Smith recommend?

690 That a $1,000 gold medal be given to Captain Rostron on behalf of the American people.

U.S. Senate inquiry

Wasn't there an inquiry in Britain as well?

 Yes. The British Board of Trade also held an investigation that began on May 2 and continued until July 3. The presiding judge was Lord Mersey, Sir John Charles Bigham.

What questions did the British inquiry attempt to answer?

Answers #692 – 695

The British Board of Trade brought up many of the same questions asked at the American inquiry, but also tried to determine the following:
● How safe was the ship?
● What ice warnings had been received?
● Were those in third class prevented from reaching the lifeboats?
● Did the *Californian* ignore the *Titanic*'s distress signals?

How many witnesses were questioned?

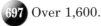 **696** Ninety-seven.

How many questions were asked of Lightoller?

697 Over 1,600.

Who were the most famous witnesses at the inquiry?

698 Sir Cosmo and Lady Duff Gordon. The newspapers had played up the fact that they had escaped in a lifeboat with only three other passengers and seven crewmen. Sir Cosmo had offered each of the crewmen £5 ($25) to help them replace their belongings. To some people this looked as if he had bribed the crew into rowing away from those who were drowning. The inquiry concluded that they were not to blame, but their reputations were damaged by the bad publicity.

What did the inquiry conclude about J. Bruce Ismay's behavior?

699 They did not find fault with his conduct.

What did they decide were the reasons for the disaster? *Answers #700 – 702*

● The ship was traveling at an excessive speed.
● A proper watch was not kept.
● The lifeboats were not properly manned.

Why didn't they say there weren't enough lifeboats?

703 Because the inquiry was conducted by the British Board of Trade which had not updated its own regulations about the number of lifeboats that ships were required to carry.

Did they think the third-class passengers had been treated unfairly?

704 No.

What did the inquiry say about the *Californian*?

705 Lord Mersey concluded that the *Californian* "might have saved many if not all of the lives that were lost."

Why wasn't the White Star Line blamed for the *Titanic*'s sinking?

706 The Board of Trade feared that this would result in lawsuits that would hurt the line's profits, damage the reputation of British shipping, and cause thousands of customers to switch to German or French liners.

What recommendations did it make?

Answers #707 – 710
● Watertight compartments should be further divided.
● Lifeboat accommodation should be provided for all on board.
● Lookouts should have regular eye tests.
● Ships should slow down and alter course when ice is reported.

AFTERMATH

How many of the *Titanic*'s passengers survived?

711 Of 329 first-class passengers, 130 were lost and 199 survived.

712 In second class, 166 of the 285 passengers were lost, while 119 survived.

713 In third class, 536 of the 710 aboard were lost, while 174 survived. (Note: These numbers are approximate, see p. 27.)

How many *Titanic* crew members survived?

714 Only 214. Of the 899 crew members on board, 685 died.

LOST **FIRST CLASS** **SAVED**

119 Men — 54 Men
11 Women and Children — 145 Women and Children
Total: 130 — Total: 199

SECOND CLASS

142 Men — 15 Men
24 Women and Children — 104 Women and Children
Total: 166 — Total: 119

THIRD CLASS

417 Men — 69 Men
119 Women and Children — 105 Women and Children
Total: 536 — Total: 174

CREW

682 Men — 194 Men
3 Women — 20 Women
Total: 685 — Total: 214

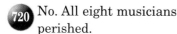

How many children lived and how many died?

Answers #715 – 717	Total	Saved	Lost
● First Class	5	4	1
● Second Class	22	22	0
● Third Class	76	23	53

Did any of the orchestra members survive?

720 No. All eight musicians perished.

Did any of the bellboys, liftboys, or pageboys survive?

721 No.

What city was hit the hardest?

722 Southampton, England, where many of the crew lived. On one street alone, 20 families were bereaved.

Who was the only child from first class to die?

718 Two-year-old Loraine Allison of Montreal.

Did any members of the Sage family survive?

719 No. All nine children (see p. 20) died with their parents.

Did the White Star Line help the families of the dead crew members?

723 No. The crew members were "casual" labor and their families had no claim to any compensation.

Did anyone help them?

724 Yes. The British Titanic Relief Fund and other British charities raised £450,000 ($2,250,000) to help the families of passengers and crew hardest hit by the disaster. In the United States, $261,000 was raised.

A memorial service for the Titanic's victims was held at St. Paul's Church in Halifax on April 21, 1912.

Didn't anyone sue the White Star Line?

725 Because the company was not found negligent by the British inquiry, passengers could only sue for damages in the United States. The total amount of all the claims came to almost $17 million. This included $50 by Eugene Daly for a set of bagpipes, $750 by Robert Daniel for his champion bulldog, Gamon de Pycombe, and $5,000 by William Carter for his new Renault. The final amount distributed to all those making claims was $663,000.

Is it true that some of the men who survived the *Titanic* were shunned?

726 Yes. Many thought it was cowardly or "unmanly" for them to have survived when so many had died.

Did more passengers die on the *Titanic* than on any other ship before or since?

Answers #727 – 729
● In 1912 the sinking of the *Titanic* was the greatest marine disaster in history. But on May 29, 1914, the *Empress of Ireland* sank in the St. Lawrence River causing the death of 840 passengers, eight more than had died on the *Titanic*. The total death toll of 1,012, however, was less.
● On January 30, 1945, the *Wilhelm Gustloff*, a ship carrying German refugees, was torpedoed by a Russian submarine off the coast of Poland and over 7,000 passengers perished.
● On December 21, 1987, the ferry *Dona Paz* collided with a tanker in the Philippines, bursting into flames and sinking within minutes. It was designed to carry 1,550 passengers, but may have had 4,000 on board. No one survived.

A 1914 illustration from a French magazine shows lifeboats searching the wreckage for **Empress of Ireland** *survivors.*

APRÈS LA CATASTROPHE DE L'"EMPRESS-OF-IRELAND"
La recherche des victimes

How many lifeboats are ships required to carry today?

730 Due in part to the *Titanic*'s tragic loss of life, modern cruise ships are required to have enough lifeboats to carry 25 percent more people than the total number of passengers and crew on board.

What is the International Ice Patrol?

731 The International Ice Patrol, under the direction of the United States Coast Guard, was created in 1914. The officers locate, mark, and track iceberg movements in the shipping lanes of the northwest Atlantic.

Have any lives been lost due to ice in the North Atlantic since the *Titanic* disaster?

732 No.

What does the United States Coast Guard / International Ice Patrol do every April 15?

Each year the U.S. Coast Guard drops a wreath from an airplane over the Titanic's final resting place.

733 Members drop a wreath provided by the Titanic Historical Society at approximately the spot where the *Titanic* went down.

WHATEVER HAPPENED TO...?

How many *Titanic* survivors are alive today?

734 In June of 1998, five are still alive, including Millvina Dean, who was two months old in April, 1912, and Michel Navratil, one of the *Titanic* "orphans," who was three.

What happened to the young people who survived the *Titanic*?

735 **Trevor Allison**, Loraine's baby brother, died of food poisoning in 1929 at the age of 18.

736 **Ruth Becker** became a teacher after marrying and raising a family. She didn't speak about her experiences on the *Titanic* until after her retirement. In 1990, she made her first sea voyage since 1912, a cruise to Mexico, and died later that year at the age of 90.

Ruth Becker in her eighties

737 **Billy Carter** became a successful businessman in Philadelphia and died there in 1985.

738 **Frank Goldsmith** went to school in Detroit, making his father's dream of a new life in the United States come true. He married, had three sons of his own, and wrote a book about his experiences on the *Titanic*. He died in 1982 and his ashes were scattered on the ocean where the *Titanic* sank.

Frank Goldsmith

739 **Eva Hart** returned to England with her mother following her father's death on the *Titanic*. After a career as an industrial welfare officer and magistrate, she died in 1996 at the age of 91.

740 **Edmond and Michel Navratil.** Edmond became an architect and builder. He served in the French army in the Second World War and escaped from a German prisoner-of-war camp, but died at the age of 43. Michel became a professor of psychology and in his old age traveled to Halifax to visit the grave of his father.

741 **Douglas Spedden** was killed in an automobile accident on August 8, 1915. He was nine years old.

Douglas Spedden

742 **Jack Thayer** graduated from the University of Pennsylvania, had a successful banking career, and later returned to his university as treasurer. In 1945, upset over his son's death in the war, he took his own life.

Jack Thayer

743 **R. Norris Williams** put the legs he saved on the *Carpathia* to good use. He entered Harvard and continued his tennis career and by the mid-1920s had twice won national singles and doubles championships.

R. Norris Williams

What happened to J. Bruce Ismay?

744 Ismay was unable to keep his job as managing director of the White Star Line because he was so unpopular with the public. Until his death in 1937, he saw very few people and no one was allowed to mention the *Titanic* in his presence.

What happened to the surviving officers and crew?

745 **C.H. Lightoller** was never made the captain of any White Star ship but did become a commander in the Royal Navy during the First World War. Later, he became a successful chicken farmer, and during the Second World War he bravely used his own yacht to bring soldiers across the English Channel from Dunkirk after the fall of France. He died in 1952.

746 **Harold Lowe**, the *Titanic*'s Fifth Officer, also never became a captain. He eventually returned to his hometown in Wales and died in 1944.

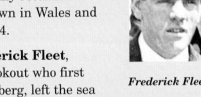

Frederick Fleet

747 **Frederick Fleet**, the lookout who first saw the iceberg, left the sea in 1936 and worked as a night watchman. Depressed over his wife's death, he committed suicide in 1965.

748 **Robert Hichens'** behavior in Lifeboat No. 6 was condemned at the U.S. inquiry by several passengers. As the man who had steered the *Titanic* into the iceberg, his career choices were limited. He eventually became the harbor master in Cape Town, South Africa.

749 **Harold Bride** was a wireless operator on a small steamer during the First World War and later became a salesman in Scotland, where he died in 1956.

Harold Bride

What about Captain Rostron?

750 He was awarded medals for his heroism and eventually became Commodore of the entire Cunard fleet.

Captain Rostron

And Captain Lord?

751 Stanley Lord was forced to resign from the Leyland Line after the British inquiry, but he enjoyed a long career as a captain with the Nitrate Producers Steam Ship Company. Several books have been written defending his actions and today his defenders (known as "Lordites") believe he was made a scapegoat.

Captain Lord

What about Mrs. Astor?

752 Madeleine Astor gave birth to a son in August 1912 and named him after his father. Although she had inherited the use of the Astor mansions and an income from a $5 million trust fund so long as she remained single, she gave it all up to remarry.

And Molly Brown?

753 Margaret Brown's bold actions in Lifeboat No. 6 led her to be accepted, for a short time, by Denver society. Sadly, it was only after her death that she gained the recognition she had always wanted with a Broadway musical and movie entitled *The Unsinkable Molly Brown*.

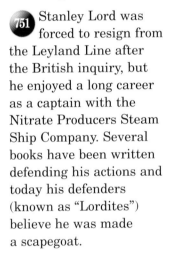

Molly Brown

WHAT HAPPENED *to the TITANIC'S* SISTER SHIPS?

White Star Line R. M. S. Olympic

F. G. O. Stuart. 1810

Is it true the *Olympic's* crew refused to sail in her after the *Titanic* disaster?

754 Yes. As the *Olympic* was about to leave Southampton on April 24, 1912, for its first Atlantic crossing since the *Titanic's* loss, its stokers went out on strike. They refused to work on a ship without enough lifeboats.

Were passengers nervous about sailing on the *Titanic's* sister ship?

755 Yes. Bookings for the *Olympic* were well down in the spring and summer of 1912. So White Star decided to take her out of service for an extensive renovation.

What changes did White Star make to the *Olympic* to persuade people to travel on it again?

Answers #756 – 758

● Her double bottom was extended up the sides to make an inner skin for the hull.

● Five of the bulkheads dividing the watertight compartments were raised to B-deck level.

● Forty-eight lifeboats were added for a total of 68.

Is it true the *Olympic* served in the First World War?

759 Yes. It became a troopship carrying a total of 119,000 Canadian and American soldiers across the Atlantic. It survived four submarine attacks, rammed and sank a German U-boat, and earned the nickname "Old Reliable."

The Olympic *painted in camouflage as a troopship*

How long did the *Olympic* sail?

760 Until 1935. During the Great Depression of the 1930s, both the White Star and Cunard lines were forced to merge and after that, the aging *Olympic* wasn't needed. In March of 1935 it made its last crossing and, before the ship was scrapped, its furnishings and fittings were sold at auction.

Was the third sister ship really going to be called *Gigantic*?

761 Yes. White Star denied this and some historians dispute it, but it is generally believed that after the *Titanic* sank, White Star decided that the *Gigantic* would be called the *Britannic*.

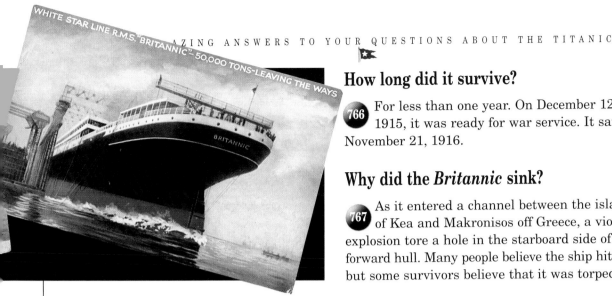

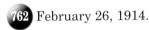

How long did it survive?

766 For less than one year. On December 12, 1915, it was ready for war service. It sank on November 21, 1916.

Why did the *Britannic* sink?

767 As it entered a channel between the islands of Kea and Makronisos off Greece, a violent explosion tore a hole in the starboard side of the forward hull. Many people believe the ship hit a mine, but some survivors believe that it was torpedoed.

When was the *Britannic* launched?

762 February 26, 1914.

Was it to be the grandest ship of the three sisters?

763 Yes. Its interiors were going to be even more lavish than the *Titanic*'s, with more wood paneling and a grand staircase that featured a huge pipe organ.

Was it also going to be the safest ship?

764 Yes. It had huge lifeboat davits that could carry six boats each, a watertight "double skin," the latest watertight doors, and higher bulkheads that could keep her afloat with any six of the ship's compartments flooded.

Did it ever carry any paying passengers?

765 No. With the outbreak of the First World War, it was converted to a hospital ship.

How did they try to save the ship?

768 Captain Charles Bartlett ordered the watertight doors closed, but the door between boiler rooms 5 and 6 failed to close properly and soon both rooms were flooded. As the ship's first six forward compartments began filling, he ordered the engines full ahead and tried to beach the ship on the nearby shore. This only increased the amount of water flooding into the compartments and the ship sank in 55 minutes.

Why did another "unsinkable" ship sink?

769 Its safety features weren't designed to cope with a mine or torpedo attack. It has also been suggested that portholes left open against orders might have speeded up the flooding of the ship.

Is it true a *Titanic* survivor was also on the *Britannic*?

770 Yes. Violet Jessop, who had been a stewardess on the *Titanic* (and on the *Olympic* when it collided with the *Hawke*), was a nurse on the *Britannic*. After the explosion she boarded a lifeboat, but it was sucked into the *Britannic*'s still-turning propellers. She jumped into the water, but as she tried to swim up to the surface her head hit the bottom of a lifeboat. Luckily, someone grabbed her and she was eventually pulled into another lifeboat.

How many people died in the sinking of the *Britannic*?

771 Only 30 of the more than 1,100 on board died, most of them in the two lifeboats that were dashed to pieces in the ship's propellers. Fortunately, unlike its sister ship, the *Britannic* was close to shore and within easy reach of rescue ships.

Where is the *Britannic* today?

772 It lies in 350 feet (107 m) of water in the Aegean Sea. It was visited in 1976 by Jacques Cousteau and explored in 1995 by Dr. Robert Ballard, the same man who discovered the *Titanic*.

DISCOVERY

Did people always want to raise the *Titanic*?

773 In March of 1914, less than two years after the sinking, a Denver inventor published a plan to raise the *Titanic* using a submarine and powerful electromagnets. Over the years many schemes were hatched to raise the ship—from creating giant winches to crank the liner up to the surface to filling the hull with thousands of Ping Pong balls. But none of them was practical.

Were there many attempts to find the *Titanic* wreck?

774 A Texas oil millionaire named Jack Grimm funded three expeditions in 1980, '81 and '83 to search for the *Titanic*. Although they searched the area around where the *Titanic* was reported to have sunk, they found nothing.

When was the *Titanic* finally discovered?

775 The *Titanic* was found on September 1, 1985.

Who discovered it?

776 A French/American team headed by underwater geologist Dr. Robert Ballard of the Woods Hole Oceanographic Institution.

(Top) Jack Grimm after his search in 1981. Jean-Louis Michel (above, left), the head of the French exploration team, and Robert Ballard aboard **Le Suroit** *(middle) in July, 1985.*

How did they find it?

777 A French team on board the ship *Le Suroit* surveyed three-quarters of the search area for one month using side-scan sonar, but found no sign of the *Titanic*.

778 In the second phase, the Woods Hole team, aboard the research ship *Knorr,* tried a different strategy. Robert Ballard knew that sinking ships leave a long trail of debris on the ocean floor. Because the debris trail would cover a bigger area than the ship itself, it would be easier to find. Starting south of where the lifeboats were picked up by the *Carpathia,* he ran his video-camera sled in wide arcs over the area.

What did they do after they realized they had found the *Titanic*?

780 Ballard and his team celebrated. Then they held a brief memorial service for all those who had died on the *Titanic*.

Robert Ballard (far right) celebrates the discovery with his team.

What did they realize when their video cameras passed over the wreck?

781 That the funnels were missing and the ship was in two pieces.

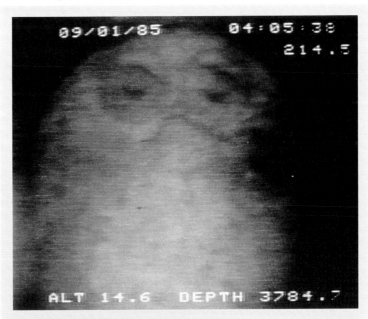

A 1911 photograph (below) of a Titanic boiler being assembled in the shop helped identify the first object the discoverers saw (above).

What was the first thing they saw?

779 Just after midnight on September 1, 1985, scattered bits of wreckage began to appear on the *Knorr*'s monitor screens. Suddenly they saw a large, round object. It was a boiler just like those used on the *Titanic*.

How deep is the wreck?

782 The water where the *Titanic* lies is 12,460 feet (3,798 m) deep.

Did they dive down to it in a submarine?

783 Not until the next year. On July 13, 1986, Robert Ballard climbed into the tiny submarine named *Alvin* for a two-and-a-half-hour descent to the *Titanic*.

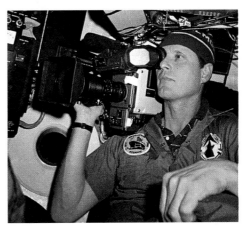

Dr. Ballard uses a hand-held video camera inside his submarine July, 1986.

EXPLORING *the* WRECK

What was it like when they first saw the *Titanic* up close?

784 Robert Ballard later described it as "an apparently endless slab of black steel" rising out of the ocean's bottom.

What are "rusticles"?

785 "Rusticles" are what Ballard called the long fingers made of rust that hang from the *Titanic*'s hull. They are formed as bacteria eats away at the iron in the ship's hull, leaving behind a waste product of reddish-brown rust particles.

In Robert Ballard's first glimpse of the wreck, he saw a wall of steel plates rising from the seafloor.

What happened to the wood on the *Titanic*?

786 Wood-boring molluscs ate most of the softer material on the wreck. After gorging themselves on the pine decks, these wormlike creatures moved inside the ship to devour everything from the furniture and paneling to the tapestries and carpets.

What is *Jason Junior*?

787 *Jason Junior,* or *JJ,* is a small remote-controlled robot connected to *Alvin* by a cable. It was able to take pictures of the *Titanic.*

Did *JJ* go inside the *Titanic*?

788 On the third of his 11 dives, Ballard parked *Alvin* near the collapsed dome of the forward Grand Staircase and sent *JJ* down the staircase shaft as far as B-deck.

What did they see?

789 *JJ* photographed the carved oak bases of some of the pillars and a light fixture. The light was still hanging from its cord.

What remained on the bow section of the ship?

Answers #790 – 796

- The anchors and anchor chains
- The fallen foremast with the crow's nest still on it
- The telemotor on the bridge that once held the ship's wheel
- The bow railing
- The gymnasium with the remains of the mechanical horse
- Ghostly davit arms and portholes
- Captain Smith's cabin

How far away is the stern section?

797 The bow and stern are 1,970 feet (600 m) apart and face in opposite directions.

What types of objects were in the debris field?

Answers #798 – 803

Near the stern lay thousands of items that spilled out of the ship's hull when it broke in half. These include:
● A porcelain doll's head for an expensive doll that could have belonged to Loraine Allison or another child in first class;

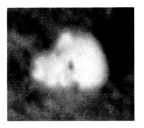

A ghostly doll's head (left) and a deck bench (middle) were among the objects found. This light fixture (right) still hangs near the Grand Staircase.

● A deck bench from the poop deck like one that Frank Goldsmith would have sat on;
● Sinks similar to the one that would have been in Ruth Becker's cabin;
● A metal footboard from a bed similar to the ones Jack Thayer or the Carter children might have slept in;
● A statue of a Greek goddess from the fireplace in the first-class lounge;
● A safe with a shiny brass crest. When *Alvin*'s arm lifted it, they saw that it was missing its back.

What remains on the stern?

804 The stern section literally blew apart on hitting the bottom. The high-pressure cylinders from the reciprocating engines and one of the cargo cranes remain, and the three propellers are still there, half-buried in the mud.

Were there any skeletons at the site?

805 No. Any bodies carried to the seabed with the wreck were eaten by fish and crustaceans. But they did see pairs of shoes where bodies once lay.

What animals have found a home in the wreck?

806 Creatures inhabiting the *Titanic*'s hull include Galathean crabs, starfish, sponges, anemones, and rat-tail fish.

What mysteries were solved by exploring the wreck? *Answers #807 – 809*

Certain long-held beliefs were disproven or confirmed, such as:
● There was no 300-foot (92-m) long gash in the hull. The iceberg popped the riveted plates.
● The calculated position for where the ship went down was incorrect. The wreck was found 13½ miles (22 km) from there.
● The ship had indeed broken in half while sinking as Jack Thayer and others had claimed.

LAST RESTING PLACE

What did Ballard leave on the wreck?

810 Ballard and his team left behind two commemorative plaques: one on a bow capstan asking all future explorers to leave the ship in peace, and one on the poop deck in memory of those who were lost.

Did Ballard take anything from the wreck?

811 No. He thought it was a grave site and should be left undisturbed.

(Above) Connected by its tether to the submarine, Jason Junior lights up the Titanic's starboard anchor. (Inset) The commemorative plaque that Ballard placed on the bow.

Have others taken things from the wreck?

Answers #812 – 818
Yes. Salvaging expeditions in 1987, 1993, and 1994 have taken hundreds of items from the site. These include:

● Bottles
● Dishes
● Light fixtures
● Luggage

● A statue of a cherub from the aft Grand Staircase
● The crow's-nest bell
● A valise containing coins, currency, and jewelry

Among the items taken from the site were a cherub statue (above) and numerous pieces of White Star china (right).

Was a safe found?

819 Although a safe was recovered on the '87 expedition, it turned out to be empty.

How did survivors react to the salvage?

820 Eva Hart was upset that what she thought of as her father's grave had been disturbed. She called the salvagers "fortune hunters, vultures, pirates."

What did a 1991 expedition do?

821 A Soviet and Canadian expedition filmed the wreck for an IMAX (large screen) documentary called *Titanica*. Scientists studied the deep-sea life and took samples of the sediment as well.

What other expeditions have been to the wreck?

822 In 1995, director James Cameron filmed the wreck for his movie *Titanic*. An expedition by RMS *Titanic,* Inc. to raise a piece of the hull plating failed in 1996 but was successful in 1998.

This safe, actually missing its back, was lifted from the debris field and "opened" on TV after the 1987 salvage expedition.

Who owns the *Titanic*?

823 The ship lies in international waters. RMS Titanic, Inc. has the rights to salvage it.

Will the *Titanic* ever be raised?

824 It's unlikely. The bow section buried itself more than 60 feet (18 m) in the mud when it slammed into the sea floor. The stern section would likely crumble into pieces if anyone attempted to move it.

TITANIC: *the* MOVIE

Where was most of the movie shot?

827 Twentieth Century Fox built a motion-picture studio for the movie on 40 acres (16 ha) of waterfront property south of Rosarito in Baja California, Mexico.

What cost more in today's money—the ship or *Titanic*?

825 The movie. The approximate cost to make *Titanic* was $200 million, while it would cost about $123 million in today's dollars to build the ship.

What else did James Cameron do on *Titanic* besides direct it?

826 He wrote the script and co-produced and co-edited the movie. He also drew all of Jack's drawings.

Was the movie's ship as large as the *Titanic*?

828 It was full scale but some parts of the ship were eliminated so that the set would fit in the 17-million-gallon (64-million-L) tank. Only the starboard side of the ship was built. When James Cameron wanted to show events happening on the port side, his cast put on clothes that buttoned the wrong way or uniforms with reversed lettering. Then the film was flopped and the scene looked normal again.

Were all the scenes of the *Titanic* wreck shot at the real wreck?

829 No. On the days that they were filming the wreck, the amount of dead plankton in the water reduced the visibility to 35 feet (11 m) at most. This meant they were unable to shoot large, wide shots of the wreck. A 1/20th scale model of the wreck was built and shots of it were used in addition to the real underwater footage. However, the fireplace shown in the wreck scenes in the movie was filmed in an actual parlor suite.

Were the rooms the same as on the *Titanic*?

830 Amazingly so. Details of the plaster-work, woodwork, light fixtures, and furniture were all faithful to the originals.

How did they flood the Grand Staircase and dining saloon?

831 They were built nearly lifesize at the bottom of an interior tank, which was then flooded with 5 million gallons (190 million L) of sea water.

Did the Heart of the Ocean really exist?

832 No, but there was some expensive jewelry on board. Lady Duff Gordon, for example, had brought along a $50,000 pearl necklace on loan from her jewelers in Venice. It was kept in the purser's safe and went down with the ship.

Was there a real Jack Dawson?

833 No. The character played by Leonardo DiCaprio isn't based on a real person. The grave marked "J. Dawson" in Halifax's Fairview Cemetery belongs to 23-year-old James Dawson, a trimmer of the *Titanic*'s crew.

Was there a real Rose DeWitt Bukater?

834 No, but the character's mother, Ruth, resembles Emily Ryerson and Marian Thayer, both wealthy Philadelphia society ladies.

Who were some of the real passengers portrayed in the dinner-party scene?

Answers #835 – 838
- Molly Brown (Kathy Bates)
- J. Bruce Ismay (Jonathan Hyde)
- Thomas Andrews (Victor Garber)
- Countess of Rothes (Rochelle Rose)

Was the "I'm the king of the world" scene true to life?

839 No. Passengers weren't allowed on the forecastle, much less right at the prow. They could, however, use the forward well deck.

On the real *Titanic*, could Jack have moved so easily between third and first class?

840 No. Gates prevented third-class passengers from entering other areas of the ship, although there were railings in parts of the ship that could be climbed over as Jack did in the movie.

Did First Officer William Murdoch really shoot himself?

841 Although some survivors said he did, Second Officer Lightoller and others who knew Murdoch didn't think so. As his body was never recovered, there is no way of knowing for sure.

How many Academy Awards did the movie win?

842 Nominated for 14 Oscars, the movie won 11.

Kate Winslet at the 1998 Academy Awards (inset) and at the Golden Globe Awards with James Cameron and Leonardo DiCaprio

What are some of the other famous movies about the *Titanic*?

Answers #843 – 845
- *Saved from the Titanic* (1912) starred first-class survivor Dorothy Gibson, a silent movie actress (see p. 34).
- *Titanic* (1953), starring Barbara Stanwyck and Clifton Webb, featured a mix of real and fictional characters.
- *A Night to Remember* (1958) was the most authentic of all the old *Titanic* movies. Its 30 interior sets were constructed from actual *Titanic* blueprints.

TITANIC: TRUE *or* FALSE?

Answers #846 – 857

No one talked about the *Titanic* as being unsinkable until after it sank.

False. It's true that White Star never advertised the *Titanic* as being unsinkable. It's true that after the sinking the newspapers played up the irony of the ship's "unsinkability." But a 1911 nautical magazine described the ship's system of watertight bulkheads and doors as making it "practically unsinkable" and people came to believe this. One Canadian passenger wrote to his mother that he was coming home on the *Titanic*, "a new unsinkable ship."

The Olympic *(left) and the* Titanic *in March, 1912*

The *Titanic* was really the *Olympic*.

False. One recent book claims that the two ships were switched by the White Star Line as part of an insurance scam. But the two ships were not identical. Unlike the *Olympic*, the *Titanic* had an enclosed forward promenade that can be seen on the wreck today. And the identification number 401 was stamped onto parts of the *Titanic* by Harland & Wolff. Expeditions to the wreck site have found the number 401 on the helm indicator and a propeller.

Men dressed as women to get into lifeboats.

False. Exaggerated stories of this were reported in the newspapers at the time and plagued many male survivors for the rest of their lives. Only one young Irish man, Daniel Buckley, admitted to wearing a woman's shawl over his head. He had jumped into Boat No. 4 along with some other men, but when they were ordered out, Daniel started to cry. He later said that Mrs. Astor threw a shawl over his head. The boat was lowered with Daniel safely aboard.

A woman divorced her husband for getting off the *Titanic* before she did.

Possibly true. Billy and Lucile Carter's mother divorced their father in 1914. He stepped into Collapsible C at about the same time his wife and children were being lowered in Boat No. 4. Like many male survivors, Mr. Carter was called cowardly and "unmanly" for having survived when so many other men had died. The shame of being married to a man who had escaped the *Titanic* may have been a factor in the divorce.

Mrs. Carter

A passenger said, "It will take more than an iceberg to get me out of bed."

True. Canadian passenger Hugo Ross was lying ill in his cabin and reportedly said this when told of the collision. He then went back to sleep. Ross did not survive.

There was an Egyptian mummy on board that caused the tragedy.

False. There is a much-repeated story about a mummy that had a curse on it and caused tragedy wherever it went. It was supposedly being shipped to New York on the *Titanic*. But there is not a shred of evidence to support the story. It has been claimed that journalist W.T. Stead told a group of friends a "ghost story" about such a mummy. Since Stead went down with the ship, this tale over time may have become repeated as "fact."

The *Titanic* was sunk by an explosion rather than the iceberg.

False. This theory was put forward by those who salvaged artifacts from the wreck in 1987. They noticed large ruptures on either side of the bow section and claimed that they had been caused by an explosion perhaps ignited by the coal bunker fire (see p. 23). But the holes on either side of the wreck are in the cargo areas and well above the waterline. They were caused when the bow bent downward after striking the bottom.

The safes were full of jewelry when the ship went down.

True. Purser Herbert McElroy encouraged passengers who came to his office demanding their jewelry to return to their staterooms for their life jackets.

The *Titanic*'s hull shattered when it hit the iceberg.

False. Some experts who studied the steel hull plates found that they had a high carbon content and theorized that they would shatter at cold temperatures. But recent investigation on the wreck has confirmed Robert Ballard's belief that the rivets popped during the collision with the iceberg.

There was a large shipment of gold aboard.

Most likely false. The cargo manifest does not list a large gold shipment. But such shipments were often sent through the mail by the Bank of England, which traded gold with the United States. Records concerning this, however, will not be opened until 2012.

A woman later claimed to be Loraine Allison and to have survived the *Titanic*.

True. A woman named Loraine Kramer appeared on a radio show in 1940 claiming that she was really Loraine Allison (see p. 53). She told an amazing story about how she had survived, and hired a lawyer to help her make a claim for the Allison estate. She persisted with this claim for ten years before giving up. Some people think she may have been supplied with Allison family memories by former nursemaid Alice Cleaver (see p. 34).

Since the movie *Titanic*, cruise ships have had to ask passengers not to stand at the tip of the bow.

True. Apparently too many passengers have been trying to imitate Jack and Rose during their vacations.

TITANIC LEGACY

What happened to the *Titanic*'s lifeboats?

858 No one knows for sure. After they were dropped off at the White Star pier by the *Carpathia*, the company flags and nameplates were removed from them. It's probable that they were shipped back to England on the *Olympic* and used again on other White Star ships. A 1912 photograph of the *Olympic* (right) in Southampton with lifeboats in the foreground, supports this theory.

What happened to the *Carpathia*?

859 It was torpedoed and sunk by a German submarine in July of 1918. The *Californian* was also sunk during World War One.

Are there any White Star ships left?

860 Apart from the wrecks of the *Titanic*, *Britannic*, and others on the ocean floor, the only White Star ship in existence today is the tender *Nomadic* which once ferried passengers out from Cherbourg. Now a floating restaurant, it is anchored on the Seine near the Eiffel Tower in Paris.

Where are there *Titanic* artifacts or exhibits?

Answers #861 – 869

In addition to numerous private collections that often go on display, and the touring exhibits of artifacts recovered from the wreck site on the sea floor by RMS Titanic, Inc., there are several permanent collections of *Titanic* memorabilia.

Canada
- Maritime Museum of the Atlantic (Halifax, N.S.)

United States
- Museum at Titanic Historical Society (Indian Orchard, MA)
- Marine Museum at Fall River (Fall River, MA)

England
- Maritime Museum (Southampton)
- National Maritime Museum (Greenwich)
- Merseyside Maritime Museum (Liverpool)
- Parts of the *Olympic*'s smoking room and gymnasium are in a private collection at the Crown-Berger Paint Factory in Haltwhistle.

Northern Ireland
- Ulster Folk and Transport Museum (Belfast)

Ireland
- Cobh Heritage Centre (Cobh)

*A Titanic **deck chair** on display at the Maritime Museum of the Atlantic in Halifax*

Where can I see memorials to the *Titanic?* *Answers #870 – 879*

Canada
● *Titanic* graves. These are at three cemeteries in Halifax, Nova Scotia: Fairview, Mount Olivet, and Baron de Hirsch.

United States
● Titanic Memorial Lighthouse (New York City— South Street Seaport)
● Women's Titanic Memorial (Washington, D.C.)
● Widener Library, Harvard University (Cambridge, MA)

England
● Engineers' Memorial (Southampton)
● Postal Officers' Memorial (Southampton)
● Musicians' Memorial (Southampton)
● Firemen and Crew Memorial Fountain (Southampton — Holyrood Church)
● Statue of Captain E.J. Smith (Lichfield)

Northern Ireland
● Titanic Memorial (Belfast)

The 1915 dedication ceremony for the Engineers' Memorial

Details of the **Olympic's** *interiors can still be seen today.*

What happened to the *Olympic's* lavish interiors?

880 They were auctioned off before the ship was scrapped. Today the *Olympic's* first-class lounge (which was identical to the *Titanic's*) and some of the staircase railings are part of the White Swan Hotel (left and top right) in Alnwick, England. The elegant paneling and fixtures from the à la carte restaurant now decorate an English home (above right).

Can I start a *Titanic* collection?

881 Yes. Many people interested in the *Titanic* have collections. Old postcards of the *Titanic* are highly collectible, including those that were published to commemorate the disaster. Also valued are period sheet music, china, menus, cutlery, and other souvenirs from White Star ships of the period. Dishes and other props from the movie *Titanic* are now for sale, and reproductions of other *Titanic* artifacts are also available.

Can I join a *Titanic* organization?

882 Yes. The Titanic Historical Society (P.O. Box 51053, Indian Orchard, MA 01151-0053, U.S.A.) holds regular conventions and publishes an excellent magazine, *The Titanic Commutator*.

Will we always be fascinated by the story of the *Titanic?*

882½ The story of the *Titanic* has fascinated people for most of the 20th century. Will it still interest us in the 21st century? What do *you* think?

GLOSSARY

A-deck, B-deck: The *Titanic*'s passenger decks were given the letters A through G. A-deck was the first deck below the boat deck.

aft: Toward the back of a ship.

berths: Single beds in a shared room.

boat deck: The deck of a ship on which the lifeboats are carried. On the *Titanic*, this was the top deck.

boiler: A furnace in which coal was burned to boil water and create steam, which in turn drove the ship.

bow: The front end of a ship.

bridge: A raised platform or structure toward the front end of a ship, which has a clear view ahead, and from which the ship is navigated.

bulkhead: An upright partition separating compartments on a ship.

cabin: A room on a ship.

collapsible: A wooden-bottomed lifeboat with canvas sides.

crow's nest: A lookout platform high on a ship's mast.

davits: Cranelike arms used for holding and lowering lifeboats.

debris field: The area between the separated bow and stern sections of the *Titanic* wreck where many objects from the ship were found.

fireman: Another name for a stoker on a ship.

forward: Toward the front of a ship.

funnel: A tall smokestack on a ship.

gangway: A ramp that allowed people boarding to walk from the dock onto the ship.

hold: A storage space for cargo on a ship, usually below decks.

hull: The frame or lower body of a ship that is partly below water when it is sailing.

magnesium flares: An early form of flash photography.

maiden voyage: The first voyage of a ship.

Morse code: A system of dots and dashes that represent the letters of the alphabet and numbers that can be sent by radio or by a flashing lamp.

passageway: A corridor on a ship.

poop deck: The high deck at the stern of a ship.

port: The left-hand side of a ship when facing the bow.

promenade: An upper deck, sometimes enclosed, on which passengers could stroll.

quintet: A musical group of five players.

quoits: A throwing game in which rings are thrown at an upright pin.

rivets: Pins or bolts of steel that hold metal plates together.

rockets: The *Titanic* fired flares that looked like fireworks as a sign that it was in distress.

starboard: The right-hand side of a ship when facing the bow.

stern: The rear end of a ship.

steward: A member of a ship's crew who attends to the needs of passengers.

stoker: A crew member who keeps a ship's boilers working to drive the engines.

telegraph: A circular machine with a rotating handle that sent messages from the *Titanic*'s bridge to its engine rooms.

telemotor: A device on a ship's bridge that held the ship's wheel.

trimmer: A crewman who helped keep the ship balanced. Trimmers carried coal by wheelbarrow from the bunkers to the boilers and made sure that the weight of the remaining coal was distributed evenly.

trio: A musical group of three players.

Turkish bath: A steam bath.

wireless: Another name for radio, often used in England.

RECOMMENDED READING

Exploring the Titanic
by Robert D. Ballard, 1988 (Scholastic, U.S. and U.K.; Penguin, Canada)
● Robert Ballard's gripping account of the discovery of the *Titanic* wreck.

Ghost Liners
by Robert D. Ballard with Rick Archbold, 1998 (Little, Brown and Co., U.S., Canada; Allen & Unwin, Australia)
● An expedition with Robert Ballard to the *Titanic* and the other great lost ships he has explored: the *Lusitania, Britannic, Empress of Ireland* and *Andrea Doria.*

Inside the Titanic: A Giant Cutaway Book
by Hugh Brewster, Illustrated by Ken Marschall, 1997 (Little, Brown and Co., U.S., Canada; Allen & Unwin, Australia)
● This book has large, detailed cutaway illustrations.

Finding the Titanic
by Robert D. Ballard, 1993 (Scholastic, U.S., U.K., Canada)
● The story of the sinking and finding of the *Titanic* for ages 7 to 9.

On Board the Titanic
by Shelley Tanaka. Paintings by Ken Marschall, 1996 (Hyperion, U.S.; Scholastic, Canada)
● The story as seen through the eyes of Jack Thayer and Harold Bride.

Polar the Titanic Bear
by Daisy Corning Stone Spedden. Illustrated by Laurie McGaw, 1994 (Little, Brown and Co., U.S., Canada, U.K.)
● Douglas Spedden's adventures on the *Titanic* as told by his mother with his toy bear as narrator.

Good Reference Books with an Adult Reading Level

The Discovery of the Titanic
by Dr. Robert D. Ballard, 1987 (Warner, U.S.; Orion, U.K.; Allen & Unwin, Australia)
● An in-depth account of Robert Ballard's two *Titanic* expeditions.

A Night to Remember
by Walter Lord, 1955 (Bantam Books)
● A gripping retelling of the sinking, by an author who interviewed many of the survivors.

Last Dinner on the Titanic
by Rick Archbold and Dana McCauley, 1997 (Hyperion, U.S. and Canada; Orion, U.K.; Allen & Unwin, Australia)
● This book tells all about the food on the ship, along with menus and recipes for meals served in each class.

Titanic: An Illustrated History
by Don Lynch and Ken Marschall, 1992 (Hyperion, U.S.; Penguin, Canada; Hodder and Stoughton, U.K.)
● An excellent account of the ship's life with hundreds of photographs and paintings.

The Titanic Collection: Mementos of the Maiden Voyage
From the Archives of the Titanic Historical Society (Chronicle Books, U.S. and Canada)
● A boxed collection with replicas of the *Titanic*'s menus, tickets, deck maps, and more.

Titanic Web Sites

The Official Titanic Movie Site
http://www.titanicmovie.com

Molly Brown House Museum
http://www.mollybrown.com

JASON Expedition Headquarters
http://www.jasonproject.org/expedition.html

Titanic Historical Society
http://www.titanic1.org

Titanic Games

Titanic: Adventure Out of Time
(CyberFlix)
An award-winning interactive computer game.

Prints and posters of Ken Marschall's work are available from: Trans-Atlantic Designs, Inc. P.O. Box 539 Redondo Beach, CA 90277 U.S.A. e-mail: tadesigns@aol.com

INDEX

Picture Credits

All paintings, unless otherwise noted, are by Ken Marschall.
DLC — Don Lynch Collection.
KMC — Ken Marschall Collection.
ILN — *Illustrated London News.*
THS — Titanic Historical Society.
UFT — Harland & Wolff Photographic Collection, National Museums & Galleries of Northern Ireland, Ulster Folk and Transport Museum
Cover: Background by Dan Fell. Porthole from "Titanic: Adventure Out of Time," courtesy of CyberFlix Incorporated.
Endpapers: Porthole from "Titanic: Adventure Out of Time," courtesy of CyberFlix Incorporated.
3 From " Titanic: Adventure Out of Time," courtesy of CyberFlix Incorporated.
6 (Left) DLC. (Upper right) ILN. (Lower right) UFT.
7 (Top) KMC. (Bottom) KMC.
8 (Top) Library of Congress. (Bottom) UFT.
9 (Top) UFT. (Middle) UFT. (Bottom) George Behe Collection.
10 (Top) UFT. (Middle) KMC. (Bottom) UFT.
11 UFT.
12 (Top) Corbis-Bettmann, U7326RAU-34. (Bottom) UFT.
13 (Top) UFT. (Bottom) Brown Brothers.
14 (Top) Simon Mills Collection.
15 (Top) Illustration by Jack McMaster.
16 Cork Examiner.
17 (Top) KMC. (Middle left) THS. (Middle right) KMC. (Bottom left) KMC. (Bottom right) KMC.
18 (Inset) UFT. (Bottom) The Board of Trustees of the National Museums & Galleries on Merseyside.
19 KMC.
20 (Top) DLC. (Middle) KMC. (Bottom) THS.
21 (Top right) UFT. (All others) KMC.

22 (Right) Diagrams by Jack McMaster. (Bottom) Father Browne, S. J. Collection.
23 (Bottom) KMC.
24 (Top) Mary Evans Picture Library. (Middle) KMC.
25 Corbis-Bettmann Collection, PG 13287.
26 (Top) KMC. (Bottom) Private Collection.
27 KMC.
28 (Bottom) KMC.
29 (Top) THS. (Inset) Onslow's Auctioneers.
30 (Top) KMC. (Middle) Father Browne, S.J., Collection (Bottom) KMC.
31 (Top) Brown Brothers. (Bottom) Father Browne, S.J., Collection.
32 (Top) KMC. (Middle) THS. (Bottom) Brown Brothers.
33 KMC.
34 (Left) Corbis-Bettmann, U 19758 INP. (Right) DLC.
35 (Far left) Corbis-Bettmann, VV 6030. (Left) KMC. (Right) Brown Brothers. (Far right) Corbis-Bettmann, U 128513 P&A. (Bottom) THS.
36 (Bottom) THS.
37 (Top) ILN.
38 THS.
40 (Top) THS. (Bottom) KMC.
41 (Top) George Behe Collection. (Second) ILN. (Third) THS. (Fourth) ILN.
42 (Bottom) Diagram by Jack McMaster.
43 Illustrations by Jack McMaster.
44 (Bottom) Diagram by Jack McMaster.
45 Diagram by Jack McMaster.
46 THS.
47 (Top left) *The Shipbuilder.* (Top right) ILN.
49 (Top) ILN. (Bottom) Painting by Laurie McGaw.
50 (Top) Mariners' Museum. (Bottom) DLC.
51 (Left) DLC. (Right) Barbara Kharouf Collection.
52 (Top) Hulton Picture Library. (Bottom) Illustrations by Peter Kovalik.

53 (Top) University of Pennsylvania Archives. (Middle) Mrs. R. Norris Williams Collection. (Bottom) Brown Brothers.
56 (Bottom) ILN.
57 Illustration by Jack McMaster.
58 Earl of Rothes Collection.
59 (Top) Mary Evans Picture Library. (Bottom) Corbis-Bettmann, UB4566-INP.
60 (Top) Courtesy of Mrs. Mary Lou Fenwick. (Bottom) ILN.
61 (Top) Corbis-Bettmann, U 30065, UB 4355INP1.
62 (Inset) Corbis-Bettmann.
63 (Left top) National Archives/DLC. (Left bottom) ILN. (Right) Brown Brothers.
64 (Top) THS. (Bottom) Courtesy of Mrs. Mary Lou Fenwick.
65 ILN.
66 (Top) Mary Evans Picture Library. (Bottom) Mrs. B. Hambly Collection.
67 THS.
68 (Top) Brown Brothers. (Bottom) Southampton City Museum.
69 (All) Brown Brothers.
70 (All) Public Archives of Nova Scotia.
71 THS.
72 Ken Marschall Collection.
73 ILN.
74 (Top) Illustration by Peter Kovalik. (Bottom) THS.
75 (Top) Mary Evans Picture Library. (Bottom) THS.
76 (Left top) KMC. (Left bottom) THS. (Right top) Daisy Corning Stone Spedden Collection, courtesy of Leighton Coleman III. (Right middle) University of Pennsylvania Archives. (Right bottom) Mrs. R. Norris Williams Collection.
77 (Left top) George Behe Collection. (Left middle) KMC. (Left bottom) ILN. (Right top) KMC. (Right middle) THS. (Right bottom) Corbis-Bettmann U30065.

78 (Top) KMC. (Middle) Maritime Museum of the Atlantic, KMC. (Bottom) THS.
79 Karen Kamuda Collection.
80 (Top) Photo by Anita Brosius, Lamont-Doherty Geological Observatory. (Middle) Emory Kristof © National Geographic Society. (Bottom) Emory Kristof © National Geographic Society.
81 (Top) Woods Hole Oceanographic Institution. (Middle) UFT. (Bottom left) Emory Kristof © National Geographic Society. (Bottom right) Woods Hole Oceanographic Institution.
82 (Middle) Woods Hole Oceanographic Institution.
83 (Top left) Diagram by Ken Marschall. (Bottom, left to right) Woods Hole Oceanographic Institution
84 (Left) Woods Hole Oceanographic Institution.
85 (Top) Woods Hole Oceanographic Institution. (Middle) KMC. (Bottom left) DLC.
86 'TITANIC'© 1997 Twentieth Century Fox Film Corporation and Paramount Pictures Corporation. All rights reserved.
87 Corbis-Bettmann, AFP 98057509-3. (Inset) Corbis-Bettmann, ZUA 13912475. (Bottom right) KMC.
88 (left) UFT. (Right) Corbis-Bettmann, UB 23A INP.
90 (Top) KMC. (Bottom) Maritime Museum of the Atlantic.
91 (Top left) Photograph by Peter Christopher. (Upper top right) Photograph by Peter Christopher. (Lower top right) Photograph by Ken Marschall. (Bottom) The Mariners' Museum.

Design and Art Direction:
Gordon Sibley
Design Inc.

Editorial Director:
Hugh M. Brewster
Editorial Assistance:
Ian R. Coutts and
Susan Aihoshi

Production Editor:
Susan Barrable
Production Co-ordinator:
Sandra L. Hall

Color Separation:
Colour Technologies
Printing and Binding:
G. Canale & C. S.p.A.,
Torino, Italy

882 ¹/₂ AMAZING ANSWERS *to your* QUESTIONS *about the* TITANIC
was produced by Madison Press Books,
which is under the direction of Albert E. Cummings.